C000068594

GOD'S
GRAND
GAME

GOD'S GRAND GAME

STEVEN COLBORNE

Tealight

TEALIGHT BOOKS
London, England
www.tealightbooks.com

God's Grand Game
Copyright © Steven Colborne 2019

Scripture quotations in this book have been taken from *The Holy
Bible*, New International Version (Hodder & Stoughton, 2011) and
The Holy Bible, English Standard Version (Collins, 2012). The Bible
version used for each particular reference is indicated in brackets
following the quotation.

ISBN: 978-1-9993693-1-6

British Library Cataloguing-in-Publication Data
A catalogue record for this book is available from the British
Library

Printed and bound in Great Britain by Clays Ltd, Elcograf S.p.A.

For Nicolette

(I will dance like there's nobody watching)

ORDER OF PLAY

INTRODUCTION

In this book, I'll be presenting a single big idea, and exploring that idea from a range of different angles. The big idea concerns the nature of God and His relationship with human beings and with the world in which we live.

The idea I will be presenting is simple but has profound implications. It is not only of philosophical and theological importance, but also affects issues related to everyday life, such as morality, mental health, and justice.

The heart of the idea can be put like this: *everything you do is what God is doing through you*. I will be exploring the idea that God is active and living, and is animating all activity in existence, including activity in the microcosm (such as the working of our bodies) and the macrocosm (such as the movement of planets and stars).

The idea, put simply, is that *God is in control of everything that happens.* The universe, from this perspective, can be seen as a cosmic playground, and the way in which God sovereignly unfolds all activity in existence might be fittingly described as *God's Grand Game.*

I hope you will enjoy reading about why I believe this to be true, and about the implications of understanding this perspective for our lives, our faith, and the future of humanity.

ABOUT THIS BOOK

This book contains revised and updated articles from my blog at *PerfectChaos.org*, as well as revised and updated chapters from two of my books, *The Philosophy of a Mad Man* and *Ultimate Truth: God Beyond Religion*. As such, this volume serves as a thorough overview of my writing and thought to date, but also contains a great deal of original content.

A Note on Christian Content

Throughout the book I discuss a range of key theological matters with reference to the Christian faith. This is because Christianity has played such an important role in my coming to knowledge of God, and for long periods of my life I identified as a Christian, immersing myself in Christian theology, attending a variety of churches, and studying the Bible. Where I discuss Christian doctrine, I have tried to do so with clarity and simplicity, so that non-Christian readers will not feel alienated by the content.[1] The perspectives of various other religions, as well as the scientific worldview, are discussed in the book, and my intention has been to construct a book that will be of significant interest to anyone who believes in God (in any form), or indeed to anyone who is not a believer in God but is curious about whether or not God exists.

A Note on Pronouns

Throughout the book I at times refer to God using the pronoun, 'He'. This is merely a theological convention — I believe God is of a spiritual nature and therefore doesn't have a particular gender. Using the term 'it' in relation to God fails to capture the grandeur and personal nature of the divine, which is why I have opted to use the more traditional pronoun.

. . .

Video Series

This book has been written in such a way as to accompany a series of videos, which will be published on the Steven Colborne YouTube channel.[2] For each chapter you read in this book, there will be a corresponding video providing an easily digestible summary of the key ideas. So, if you like your philosophy presented in a visual medium, I warmly invite you to visit the channel, where you can enjoy lots of free content and subscribe to be notified of future videos.

Be Sure to Get in Touch

In the final chapter of this book, I propose the creation of a new church: the church of the future. I describe a vision of an institution that exists for everyone who believes there is one God over all creation, and which will be an exciting place for theological dialogue among individuals from a wide range of faith backgrounds. If you're reading this, I'm excited to explore how you might contribute to the church. You'll find my contact details at the end of the book, and I'd be delighted to hear from you and learn about the dreams and ambitions God has given you, and how we can work together.

I'm excited to delve into philosophical matters, but first, to provide some context, I'll share a little information about my background and my spiritual journey to date.

MY JOURNEY SO FAR

My Mother and Father

I grew up in the historic town of Abingdon in Oxfordshire in the south east of England. I enjoyed the privileges of a middle-class upbringing, attending decent schools and having my practical needs met, but at the same time intense relationship problems between my mother and father affected me deeply.

My mother was an atheist and my father a Christian. My father took my sister and I to church some Sundays, where I sang in the choir. But church was always something that I considered to be boring and irrelevant; I had no real sense of the gospel at the heart of the Christian faith.

As a teenager, I was an atheist like my mother and I was very dismissive of the idea of God, believing religion to be fantasy and seeing believers as naive. I would even say that the idea of God angered me.

I became heavily involved in music, which provided a focus during my early teens. I felt a great deal of anger towards my father over the way he treated my mother and my sister and I, but I found an outlet for these difficult emotions in the energetic live shows of alternative music artists like Marilyn Manson and Rage Against the Machine. Letting off steam in the mosh pit at a rock concert was liberating, and attending music festivals was a highlight of my teenage years.

Tragedy Strikes

A turning point in my life came when my mother was unexpectedly diagnosed with an aggressive form of cancer in her early fifties. I was 17 at the time. Watching my mother suffer through a gruelling treatment regime was hugely upsetting. Her marriage to my father was already strained, but the cancer diagnosis seemed to increase hostilities and my parents eventually separated, with my mother moving back to her native country of the Netherlands as a way of escaping the hurtful relationship.

The Quest for Healing

My mother was desperate to recover, and embarked upon a spiritual journey of sorts as she sought to find alternative therapies with a view to becoming well again. She became very interested in New Age spirituality, and started following teachers such as Deepak Chopra, Brandon Bays, and Eckhart Tolle. I found a great deal of inspiration in these teachers, as they wrote about subjects such as consciousness, meditation, and the spiritual causes of disease, none of which I had explored before. For the first time in my life I developed a yearning for truth, becoming obsessed with the idea that I could attain enlightenment or self-realisation.

Death Deals a Blow

After a long and gruelling illness, my mother passed away in 2003 at the age of 55, and watching her die after being so determined to recover was deeply saddening. The full impact of my mother's death didn't hit me right away, but it was a catalyst for me spiritually; I found myself asking big questions about the meaning of life and I wanted to understand the reasons why my mother had to suffer so terribly.

My mother's illness had coincided with my time at university in London, which meant a lot of journeying back and forth between England and the Netherlands. Although I was studying Commercial Music, my deep passion for spirituality had been ignited, and I would spend hours meditating or lying in the bath listening to recordings of the comparative religion philosopher Alan Watts. Another teacher who was introduced to me by a friend at this time was Ramana Maharshi, an Indian guru who taught a method of spiritual investigation known as 'self-enquiry'.

Following my mother's death in 2003, my spiritual search became really chaotic. I went on various meditation retreats and became involved in a kind of cult led by an Indian teacher named Ratu Bagus who taught a practice known as 'shaking meditation'. I experienced turbulent mental health during this time and was full of confusion, depression, and hopelessness. The people closest to me were becoming worried about me, and with good reason; I was really struggling.

Around this time, I entered into my first serious relationship with a girl who I had met at university, and upon graduation I began my career with a fairly prestigious and well-paid job in the heart of the music industry. There were some good times, but I was also very lost spiritually, and my obsession with enlightenment eventually led me to attend psychotherapy for the first time.

Encountering a Healer

To say psychotherapy was eye-opening would be an understatement. It was as though I had for many years been seeking a guru or master or just someone who could understand me and help me, and finally, in my psychotherapist, I had found that person.

A tremendous amount of healing took place in my psychotherapy sessions, which I attended on and off for several years. I was able to process a range of difficult emotions, and to eventually come to terms with my mother's death and deal with a lot of the pain that I had bottled up during my childhood when my mother and father were fighting.

But despite being a profoundly important turning point in my life, psychotherapy did not signify the end of my spiritual and psychological struggles. In fact, the five or so years following my first psychotherapy session were probably the most turbulent of my life.

My First Breakdown

Due to a combination of stress, panic attacks, and depression, in 2007 I was forced to leave my second high-profile job in the music industry, and essentially became bed-ridden for weeks. I began to experience strange states of mind, feeling that I was caught up in grand conspiracies. My behaviour became increasingly erratic. In retrospect, I would describe this period as the onset of my first psychotic episode, though having had no experience of mental illness in my own life or the lives of those around me, I didn't consider this to be a possibility at the time.

Things got particularly out of hand one day when I threw my phone in the bin and got on a train to Gatwick Airport carrying little other than my passport. I had no idea where I was going, but I picked a flight to Italy and proceeded to have a serious panic attack on the plane. For the entirety of the flight I struggled to breathe, and when the plane finally landed I immediately got a taxi to the nearest hospital, recognising that I was in a dire state. I hadn't slept properly for weeks and the stress that I was feeling was intense. A doctor gave me just enough morphine so that I was able to sleep for half an hour and get a flight back to London the following morning.

This is just one example of a series of events that eventually led to me being sectioned under the Mental Health Act and admitted to psychiatric hospital for the first time. When I arrived on the ward, I was skin and bones (having not eaten properly for weeks), but over a period of a few weeks I began to recover somewhat with the help of regular food and medication. This spell in hospital was especially significant in my spiritual journey because I asked a member of staff for a Bible, which I began to read and take seriously for the first time, much to the surprise of friends and family who knew me as an ardent atheist.

The Paradox of Psychosis

When I reflect upon the period leading up to my

first admission to psychiatric hospital, I can recall that it was a deeply spiritual time. From days spent sleeping rough outside a mosque, to watching *The Da Vinci Code* on repeat, to binge-watching videos about New Age spirituality on YouTube, I was awakening to a deeper aspect of reality that, up until that point in my life, had simply not existed. Experiencing altered states of reality taught me a lot about the human mind and how there are dimensions to human experience I hadn't previously been aware of.

The paradox is that, while being a period of intense mental breakdown, this episode was simultaneously a period of intense spiritual awakening. I believe I learned more about God from my experiences during this time than many scholars might learn from studying theology for a lifetime.

The Cycle of Illness and Recovery

In the years following my first admission to psychiatric hospital, there were periods of stability and periods of chaos. During the more stable times I was usually still struggling with depression and the severe side effects of the antipsychotic medication I continued to take, but was able to work for periods of time despite these challenges.

A kind of cycle developed, where I would begin to find the side-effects of the medication intolerable, and so would reduce the dose gradually and then come off the medication completely, but then within a few months I would begin to experience psychosis again and end up back in hospital. This happened three times, although on each occasion the range of experiences I went through were very different from one another.

During the periods when I was more stable, I was able to engross myself in the study of philosophy and theology, even to the extent that I completed a postgraduate course in Philosophy and Religion at the University of London in 2012. I was also able to write and self-publish two books, *The Philosophy of a Mad Man* in 2012, and *Ultimate Truth: God Beyond Religion* in 2013, which expounded for the first time the philosophical perspective I had developed after more than a decade of spiritual exploration and the study of Christianity and other religions.

Blessed Stability

The brief overview presented here merely scratches the surface of my spiritual journey. There are plenty more experiences of significance that I could recall, and my book *The Philosophy of a Mad Man* discusses these in some depth. Here, I wanted to give a brief overview of my journey in order to introduce new readers to some of the major events that have shaped my life and my beliefs.

It is now nearly five years since I experienced a significant episode of mental illness, and this period of stability has been a blessed opportunity for me to immerse myself in the further study of philosophy and theology. It gives me great pleasure that I am now able to share all I have learned from my spiritual and theological adventures in the form of this book, which I hope will become a part of your own spiritual journey — if God wills it.

Without further ado, let's begin with a look at some of the reasons why I am convinced that God exists.

PART I

THE NATURE OF GOD

1

HOW DO I KNOW GOD EXISTS?

I am happy to declare that I am 100% certain that God exists. I am at least as certain that God exists as I am that I exist. I know that for those readers who have had no revelation of the reality of God, such certainty will be hard to understand and accept, but I will offer a few reasons as to why I am so confident.

I will offer two types of argument for the existence of God, which I will categorise as logical and experiential. Let's start with the logical arguments.

Firstly, I would point to the fact that there are many examples of how the activity we witness in creation is highly coordinated. Within the human body, for instance, there are millions of complex interactions working in harmony. The occurrence of such complex yet harmonious events must mean that something is able to coordinate what is going on in my heart, brain, stomach, and feet, all at the same time. That 'something' is God.

More evidence that God exists is that we grow from nothing into human beings. We never make a decision to grow from a baby to a child to an adult; something causes this process to happen. For me, scientific ideas like genetics and evolution do not explain this process of growth in a satisfying way, as they both present a view of reality where the past determines the future, which is actually not the case.[1] Instead, there is a power operating in the present moment that causes our bodily development. That power is God.

I am not convinced by the argument that the brain is a machine that powers the rest of the body, for if this were the case, what is the cause of the brain's *own* activity? You might say 'I' am causing my brain to coordinate the millions of processes that are happening in my body. But I hope you can see the absurdity of this position — you certainly cannot explain how you are controlling your brain and bodily processes.

So perhaps your brain is controlling you? This is equally absurd. How could you attribute to a lump of grey matter the ability to write symphonies or books, to plan a holiday, or to have a relationship? Any deep-thinking person must admit there is more to human life than a series of mechanical processes somehow brought about by a mass of squishy tissue.

It is obvious that I am not controlling my brain, and my brain is not controlling me. How, then, do I explain my actions? The solution is that a spiritual being, which I like to call God, is animating all the processes that lead to my experience of my body and the world in which I exist.

As well as there being sound logical arguments for God's existence, there are also experiential arguments. For instance, I am certain that God exists because God talks to me.[2] I am certain that God exists because I have witnessed and experienced many supernatural events. On one occasion, a friend of mine prayed for a stranger on the street to be healed of the pain he was experiencing throughout his body (he had crutches and was clearly suffering). Following the prayer, the man revealed, with a look of shock upon his face, that his pain had completely gone. This was an obvious sign of immediate divine intervention. And I have witnessed many such healings.

I fully understand that if God hasn't given you a revelation of His reality then, of course, you will not believe in Him. I used to be an atheist and was happy to direct ridicule towards the apparent fairy tales of faith. But I am a living testimony of the fact that God reveals Himself to people unexpectedly, and that it's possible for anyone to go from 100% atheist to 100% theist.

At the present time I enjoy an intimate personal relationship with God, which involves conversation on a daily basis and an awareness of His existence almost continually. If you're a sceptic you may question the veracity of these experiences, but that will all change one day if you are fortunate enough to have the living God reveal Himself to you too.[3]

In the next chapter, we will look a little more closely at the idea that God is coordinating all activity in existence.

2

THE COSMIC ANIMATOR

Wherever there is activity in the universe, there must be a power that is causing that activity. Even scientists, who are very successful in describing *how* things happen, generally agree that they cannot say *why* things happen. The answer to the *why* question is that there is an all-powerful cause of everything that happens. This cause is not a scientific law or set of laws, but is the cause of the activity that allows scientific laws to be formulated. The existence of this power cannot be proven with equations but is knowable by intuition if one rationally considers the nature of activity in the cosmos.

Because one of the attributes of God is infinite correlation (God can do an infinite number of things simultaneously), God can coordinate activity in the microcosm and the macrocosm. He can make all the hairs on your head grow at the same time, and can move your arms around at the same time as He pumps blood through those arms. God can make your heart beat while you walk along the road and hold a conversation.

On a larger scale, God can create communities, ecosystems, and the orbits of celestial bodies. All of these occurrences happen in harmony, and I believe they can only be understood in terms of the coordinating power of God, who is actively controlling the existence of all things.

In order for me to clarify exactly what I mean when I am referring to God, in the next chapter we will look at a few of God's attributes.

3

WHAT ARE GOD'S ATTRIBUTES?

Over the centuries, philosophers and theologians have often struggled to understand the nature of the God who we so often discuss. God doesn't reveal His nature to everyone all the time; instead, different people are given different understandings and insights into the way God is, and they receive these at different times in their lives, and throughout history.

I believe that God intentionally limits our experience of Him, so that it is only ever partial and incomplete during human life. This is all part of the game of life, which is the way God chooses to use the infinite power which is at His disposal. God creates people of all different faiths and no faith, in order to present a vast spectrum of experience, and to give expression to some of the infinite possibilities that are contained within His nature.

At this moment in my life, I can confidently say that God has given me an awareness of His existence. I believe that God could take that awareness away at any time and change my beliefs, but for the time being, at least, it seems that God wants me to know He exists and to write about Him.

I can confidently say the following things about God:

God is everywhere (omnipresent)

God has no boundaries

God is all that exists

God is creative

God is all-powerful (omnipotent)

God is all-knowing (omniscient)

God is living

God is real

God is mysterious

The above attributes go as far as I can go in defining the God that I believe in. Although I believe God's essence (ontologically speaking)[1] is love, I am unhappy with the way Christians often describe God as love, because they do so with the implication that nothing bad can come from Him. Although I believe all love comes from God, I also believe all hate comes from God.[2] Therefore, to say that God is love in the Christian sense feels rather one-sided.

In my list of God's attributes, I have included that God is 'mysterious' because there are some aspects of God's fundamental nature that remain veiled to me, and, I suspect, to all people during our lives as human beings. We lack the bigger picture of how God experiences reality.[3] It is possible that during certain peak events in our lives, or perhaps after death, we will be given a greater understanding and awareness of God's fundamental essence or nature.

I like to imagine that after death, our awareness expands and reunites with the infinite and we regain the certain knowledge that God (who is really our deeper selves) has been in control of all aspects of our lives throughout their entirety. I have experienced a glimpse of such expansive awareness in the deeper stages of meditation, so it is not difficult for me to envisage that a more intense version of this experience could play out in the event of death.

4

GOD IN INANIMATE OBJECTS

It is easy to see how God is active in living creatures, but it is perhaps somewhat more difficult to envisage what 'God is doing' in the case of inanimate objects, like tables or books. When I look at a table and investigate its nature, an obvious question arises — is God making the table be, or can the table be without involvement from God?

The table existing without involvement from God would have to mean that there is some part of the cosmos in which God is not present. But this cannot be, as God by His very nature is omnipresent. Therefore, there must be a sense in which the table is 'in God', or, put another way, God's being must permeate the table. It is natural, then, to assume that

God is holding the table in existence. The table appears solid and stable, and it is perfectly possible for God to create these qualities in the table. God is, after all, omnipotent, so holding a bunch of atoms in place for a few hundred years does not pose the slightest problem.

Another aspect of God is that He is wholly in the parts as well as the whole. This means that each individual part of the table contains the fullness of God. It should not be hard to imagine, then, that God, in His infinite power, can create subtle change in such objects over time. We are talking, for instance, of objects like the table fading in colour, becoming infested by woodworm, or drying out. If the smallest particle is just as present to God as the whole table, then God can affect change on any level.

One might naturally ask, what would become of the table if God's involvement were taken away? Could it exist without God? We have already established that God is everywhere, so we would have to conclude that there can be no table without God.

Taking all of this into account, should it not be possible for God to make major unexpected changes in the order of things? For instance, if God wanted my table to vanish before my eyes, is this not possible? Remember, we are saying that God is holding every particle of the table in existence. I would have to conclude that, yes, it is as possible for a table to vanish as it is for a man's pain to vanish, as I described witnessing in the chapter "How Do I Know God Exists?". God could remove a table from existence in a flash, if He desired. So why, then, do we not see more instances of this?

Well, it is perfectly possible that God likes order. Perhaps regularity is one of the things that gives God pleasure. This is understandable if we remember that God has all of eternity at His disposal. God might like to make some things appear and disappear (like a flash of lightning), and cause other things to remain for hundreds of years (like a table). Evolution (in objects as well as animals) may well please God, as the unfolding of His will and His plans provide our creator with anticipation and something to look forward to.

5

DETERMINISM AND THE NATURE
OF GOD

Often, technical terminology can be headache-inducing, so I typically try to avoid it. But philosophical terms can be helpful if they encapsulate something profound and meaningful that relates to our lives and our understanding of reality. I believe that *determinism* is one such term which can provoke us to think deeply about the relationship between God and creation.

In this chapter, I will offer some brief and simple definitions of a few different types of determinism. Hopefully, they will help you to understand what I am arguing in this book about God's relationship with human beings.

Scientific Determinism

Scientific determinism is the idea that events unfold in accordance with strict scientific laws, and that one event leads to another. Every event occurs due to a series of causes that preceded it. Many physicists believe that every event we experience can be traced back to a causal chain which has been set in motion with the 'Big Bang', when time itself came into existence. There is no free will in this view — only cause and effect.

Theological Determinism

Theological determinism is the idea that God has predestined the occurrence of all events and that He has been responsible for every event throughout the course of history. This idea is similar to scientific determinism except that, here, God is the originating cause of all events, rather than chance or purely physical processes. To further complicate matters, there are two main types of theological determinism: hard determinism and soft determinism.

People who take the position of hard determinism believe that God's omniscience is not compatible with human free will. God is the cause of all events, so there is no room for free will.

The view of soft determinism is compatible with a specific meaning of freedom, which is that one's behaviour is caused not only by prior events, but also by acts of the will, such as choices, decisions and desires.

What are we to make of all this? I believe the most important consideration here is one that is often overlooked in theological discussions surrounding determinism, which is *the nature of God*. Here are a few important questions that I invite you to consider, and which will be addressed throughout this book: Did God set the universe in motion and then sit back and watch it unfold at a distance, only intervening at certain times? Or is God an omnipresent being, pervading all of creation and effecting change wherever it occurs in the present moment? Is God distant or involved? Is God boundless or somehow embodied? Is God limited in any way?

Of course, for many scientific determinists, these questions about God will not even arise, for they see no 'evidence' that God exists. But for the theist, what is understood about the nature of God will lead to conclusions concerning which type of determinism — if any — is embraced.

Having briefly explored some of the different types of determinism, in the next chapter we will see why a deterministic view of reality fails to take into account the true nature of God.

6

DOES GOD HAVE FOREKNOWLEDGE?

The problem with claiming God has 'foreknowledge' is that it implies all future events are already determined. This would only be the case in a kind of clockwork universe where cause leads to effect and nothing can change the wheels that have been set in motion, presumably in the first moment of creation, as those who believe in a 'Big Bang' theory might suppose.

But does it make sense to suggest that God waved a magic wand, said 'Go!' and then reclined back on His cloud in heaven to observe the universe unfolding for all eternity? Of course not. God is not just the creator but the *sustainer* and *animator* of all things. He is working in this very moment to carry out His will. The future, although it may be planned by God, is not certain until He brings it about. God is living and He is everywhere in this single eternal moment — He is all that there is and all of existence is contained within His being.

In any moment, God can choose to unfold the next chapter of the story as He desires and according to the infinite possibilities available to Him. To deny this would be to limit His power, and I believe He is omnipotent. Those who believe in a deterministic universe must either deny God altogether, or, if they do believe in God, consider three very important questions: Who or what is God? Where is God? What is God doing right now?

As we continue to explore the way in which God is active in existence, let us now closely examine one aspect of God's nature which will give us an insight into the way He interacts with human beings and the world around us — His creativity.

7

THE CREATIVITY OF GOD

Have you noticed how the very same piece of music can have different meanings at different times?

Let's think about a hypothetical song and call it 'N'. When you first heard N, it didn't really impact you, but after a couple of listens it began to stir a feeling of excitement and joy in you. This feeling lasted for a few more plays but, after a few weeks of listening to the song, the excitement waned and you began to find N rather boring. A few years later, you heard N again and it made you feel melancholy, evoking a time in the past when your sense of self was palpably different.

What the experiences I have described above should tell us about the song is that *its meaning is not contained within the song itself but is instead located in our reaction to it.*

But what is it that causes our reaction to a piece of music? If I'm correct, and God is not only the creator but also the animator of all activity in existence, this means He is responsible for the emotions we experience when we listen to a piece of music. God is *literally* putting thoughts and feelings into our minds and bodies as we listen.

I have used the example of music in this chapter, but the same explanation could be stated for all creative works. *The meaning of a piece of art is not in the thing itself, but rather in what God brings to the piece via our reactions to it.*

Have you ever wondered why a bizarre abstract painting even qualifies as a piece of art? It's because God evokes a certain reverence for it in the minds of those who view it.

Taking this suggestion to its logical conclusion, it would be correct to say that God is behind every book, every painting, every song, every film, every opera, every theatre production, and so on. He is behind every piece of creative work — and, most importantly, every interpretation of every creative work — that has ever been made in the history of humanity. I invite the reader to consider what this demonstrates about the incredible power and creativity of God.

Of course, the examples I have given of human art only scratch the surface. I have said nothing of the plants, animals, stars, planets, foods, and an infinite number of other objects and beings that are part of God's creative work.

I find the infinite creativity of God to be truly awe-inspiring. Don't you?

8

THE ASEITY OF GOD

My greatest fascination in this life is with the area of theology known as 'divine ontology' — the nature of God's being. I actually feel quite excited whenever I direct my attention towards this subject area and ponder the immensity of the universe and what this indicates in relation to its creator.

Perhaps the one attribute of God that delights me the most is His *aseity*. Without intending to gush, the truth is I find it difficult to capture in words the extent to which I'm enthralled by this. It is a truly wonderful and awe-inspiring concept to behold.

The word aseity has Latin roots, with *a* meaning 'from', *se* meaning 'self', and *ity* meaning 'ness'. So aseity means 'from-self-ness'. To expand upon this, we might say that the word means 'self-existing', and when applied to God, it means He is uncaused or uncreated.

This is very relevant to the philosophical problem of why there is something rather than nothing. Many scientists posit that existence started with a 'Big Bang', but this theory will always beg the question of what came before. It is illogical to argue that something can emerge out of nothing. The solution to this problem is God's aseity; there has never been a time when God didn't exist, as His very nature is being.

Pondering God's aseity has led me to understand that God is not different from existence. If this is true, then everything that exists is a part of God. I'm not arguing for pantheism (which equates God with nature), for I believe the physical world could cease to exist and God, because of His aseity, would remain perfectly whole. Creation is instead contained 'within God' and this makes sense because if God is boundless then nothing can exist outside of Him.

The implications of this perspective for traditional theism, where God is seen as separate from His creation, are obvious. If there are no limits to the extent of God's being, then it logically follows that there can be no freedom from God (free will). Instead, we must see the entirety of creation as an expression of God's being, and under His control.

What I love about the concept of aseity is that, despite being a logical explanation of one of God's fundamental attributes, it is still deeply mysterious. I invite you to meditate on this concept in all its richness.

9

SOVEREIGNTY

The word 'sovereignty' can have several nuanced meanings which I would like to briefly discuss with the hope that it will help you to understand my perspective on free will and the God/world relationship.

Here in the UK, we live under the sovereignty of the monarchy. This means that the reigning monarch (presently Queen Elizabeth II) has certain powers and authority in our country and all the countries over which she is Head of State.

We have a constitution, and although most of the power in the UK rests with our elected Members of Parliament, it is still the Queen who at least in principle has the power to appoint and dismiss ministers, direct the actions of the military, regulate the civil service, issue passports, and negotiate treaties, alliances, and international agreements, for example.

So, we can see that the role of the sovereign in the UK is to make important decisions that directly affect the lives of his or her subjects. But while the sovereign may make decisions that affect the bigger picture of our country on the world stage, aside from intervention in specific circumstances the sovereign is not in control of the details of our lives.

To understand the sovereignty of God, on the other hand, we need to understand some things about His nature which are different to that of an earthly monarch. The Queen is a being with physical and mental boundaries, whereas God is boundless. The Queen has limited powers that are God-given, whereas God has unlimited power by His very nature. The Queen exists in space and time, but God is beyond these limitations. The Queen sits on a throne, whereas God is everywhere due to His omnipresence.

In emphasising these points, I aim to highlight that the type of sovereignty God has is unique and distinct from that of any earthly sovereign, so it is simply not possible to draw an accurate correlation between the two.

God is in control of all the details of our lives, whereas the Queen is not. God is the creator, sustainer, and animator of everything that is under His dominion, whereas a monarch possesses none of these qualities. In my opinion, God's sovereignty means that, ultimately, we do not possess free will, whereas a reigning human monarch leaves us with certain freedoms.

I find it unhelpful when people draw an analogy between the sovereignty of God and earthly sovereignty, because the attributes of these different types of sovereign are completely different. This is something which it is important to keep in mind when considering my worldview and my belief that God's sovereignty necessarily means we do not have free will.

Having explored some of the attributes and characteristics that are definitional of God, in Part 2 we will look at some of the ways in which God relates to the human mind.

PART II

THE HUMAN MIND AND GOD

10

GOD'S CONTROL OF MENTAL STATES

I would like to reflect briefly on what some of the experiences in my mental health journey have taught me about God. All of the episodes of psychosis that I've experienced have been very spiritual, and by this, I mean that I have experienced aspects of reality that go beyond the mundane, everyday experiences of normal life into something altogether grander and more mysterious.

In the past, I have compared the experience of psychosis to being in a computer game. The familiar people and circumstances of everyday life are transformed in their meaning and in the way one relates to them. For instance, a simple gesture like a cough or a footstep could become part of a power play to the psychotic mind. On a grander scale, when experiencing an episode of psychosis, familiar people in one's life might become altogether different in terms of their background, status, and relation to you.

What this tells us about perception is that it is something very fluid. We imagine, when we talk about our life story, that it is something concrete and real, but the experience of psychosis has taught me that what we perceive to be our 'background' or 'personality' are just particular presentations from God to the mind, which are no more tangible than the perspective one might experience in a dream.

In a dream, it is possible to experience the everyday laws of nature that we take for granted in a completely different way. For instance, in a dream, one might be able to fly or walk on the ceiling. I am going to be so bold as to suggest that what we consider to be the laws of nature in waking life are not stable in the way that is commonly assumed. For instance, on one occasion, during my first episode of psychosis, I had the experience of being drunk without having consumed any alcohol. I was walking along the street and picked up an empty bottle of whisky that was lying on the pavement. As soon as I held the bottle, a state of drunkenness came over me and I started staggering along, and then a couple of minutes later God returned my mind to its normal sober state in an instant.

The sceptic, of course, will doubt that something like this could really happen, and will question whether I am recalling the scenario accurately. But I am convinced this happened, and it showed me that the states of mind that we experience, which we imagine are linked to the external world, are actually under God's control. For instance, we imagine that hunger arises due to some 'natural' urge to sustain our bodies, but in the same way as God can make us feel drunk without alcohol, I believe He could also, if He so willed, make us hungry with a full stomach, or tired after a good sleep.

A similar thing could be said of mind-altering substances. I remember my first experience of taking the drug Ecstasy, and how it produced in me a state of intense connectedness with the world around me and a deeper awareness of everything I encountered. I honestly believe that this experience of connectedness was not caused by the pill I took, but by God altering my reality.

On a different occasion, I ate some hallucinogenic

mushrooms, and for the next few hours had the most intense fits of laughter that I have ever experienced. I cannot accept that eating a very small quantity of a fungus could be truly responsible for such an intense experience, and as with the Ecstasy, I believe there was something very deep and spiritual going on, which finds its ultimate explanation in God, rather than the substance I consumed.

I believe the fact that people often experience similar effects when taking a particular substance is due to the fact that God likes to employ regularity within the grand game of existence. While the substances themselves aren't ultimately responsible for the effects — God is responsible — the substances are still triggers in the sense that God uses them in a playful way to initiate a series of experiences which people may subsequently attribute to the substances.

While I do not endorse experimenting with such substances, I cannot deny that they gave me deep insights into the nature of reality and the way God relates to the human mind.

11

MODES OF MIND

In order to better understand how God guides every aspect of our lives, let us briefly examine what it is that constitutes our personality, our character, and our unique experience of being an individual.

Throughout each day, and throughout our lives, we experience the coming and going of what I will term *modes of mind*. These are mental experiences we have. Some are subtle and last for many days, weeks, or even years, while others may come and go in a few seconds. I believe the modes of mind that we experience are brought about by God and are the means by which He creates in us our personal uniqueness, our qualities, and our personality.

In terms of the longer-lasting modes of mind, we

may imagine such examples as our nationality, our gender, or our sexual orientation. These are with us on a daily basis and contribute significantly to how we feel about ourselves. These attributes might manifest in a certain way of speaking. For instance, if I am British, I will probably have a British accent and use certain phrases in a particular language. I might also feel more comfortable and at peace when I am in my homeland, and there are likely to be certain feelings associated with the place in which I grew up or where I went to school or college, for instance. Throughout my life, as I move to different cities and work in different environments, these modes of mind will shift.

It's interesting that when we listen to a piece of music from our past, we will often experience a feeling of nostalgia and a kind of 'emotional memory' of who we were at a certain time in the past when our modes of mind were quite different. This is evidence that these *background modes* exist, and that they shift with time.

There are also more fleeting *associative modes* of mind that we experience during specific periods in our lives: the feeling of belonging to a certain church or mosque, the feeling of being married to a spouse or having a boyfriend/girlfriend, or the feeling of being affiliated with a political party, for instance.

On an even smaller scale, there are other even more transitory modes of mind that I will call *micro modes* which also contribute to our character and our personality. Perhaps the sensation of tasting our favourite food or the feeling of listening to a song we love would be examples of these.

What I would like us to consider is that each of the modes of mind that I have described above come together in our daily experiences in order to give us our character and personality.

God may create modes of mind that are common to certain races, nations, or historical time periods. So, when we watch a film about an event in history, for instance, we may experience the modes of mind associated with the people who lived in those times. I believe that in a world where nothing is tangible and everything (except God) is necessarily fleeting, a combination of these modes of mind is God's way of creating distinct human beings with their own char-acters and personalities.

If we think deeply about what a personality is, we

can see that it is made up of certain characteristics that endure over time. I would like to include God in this, and say that our personalities are the way that God chooses to give us different modes of mind on a daily basis and throughout our lives.

The different modes of mind, far from being anything tangible and fixed, come and go as God pleases. They have no substantial existence; they are just impressions in consciousness. One of the things that experiencing psychosis taught me is that these modes of mind can change drastically, so that we can essentially become a completely different person with a different character or personality.

Another example of this happening is in the case of those who don't associate their gender with their physical form. God has given such people certain modes of mind that are unrelated to their physical form, for instance, sexual attraction, preference for a way of dressing, etc.[1]

It is important to point out that within the modes of mind that I am here describing, emotional states are also included. Our emotions and thoughts are often interlinked, and both contribute to the modes of mind that we experience throughout our lives. I should also point out that our experiences are not robotic but fluid, and the categories of modes of mind that I have described above should be understood as flowing into one another, rather than being absolutely distinguishable.

It is wonderful to see how our modes of mind change and develop throughout our lives as God unfolds our life stories. The modes we experience as a child, for instance, are very different from those that we experience as an adult. Our unique modes of mind are continually influencing others with whom we come into contact, and the modes of mind of others are affecting us, and God is directing this entire process.

In a mere moment, God can change the modes of mind that we experience and which we feel are part of our personality or character. These impressions in consciousness do not have their origin in brain states,[2] although our bodies certainly seem to play a role in our direct experience of them.

Who you are is something very fluid and intangible; you are a collection of modes of mind manifested in your evolving consciousness by the living God, who controls all things. What comes and goes (and our modes of mind do come and go) cannot ultimately be thought of as *real* — only what endures eternally is real, and only one thing endures eternally, which is God.

In the next chapter, we will look at one particular aspect of our mental experience: thought. I will demonstrate why I believe thought can only be understood in terms of the manifesting power of God.

12

WHAT IS CAUSING OUR THOUGHTS?

Let us examine closely what thought is, and let us try to decipher what it is that causes thoughts to arise in our minds.

It is clear that when we think, there is a movement within consciousness that we are aware of. An impression in the mind seems to arise out of nothing. That impression might be a word or a sentence, or an image, or something more obscure.

An interesting point to note about thought is that it appears to be spontaneous. If you are asked to think of a fruit, for instance, then one fruit rather than another will pop into your awareness quite spontaneously (try it!). You might think 'apple' or 'watermelon' without having any particular reason for thinking of the fruit you chose. It is not necessary for you to have had an apple for breakfast, for example, or to have seen a watermelon in your local store earlier that day for you to think of those particular fruits.

It seems that we never know what our next thought will be. If I asked you to tell me what you will be thinking about in a minute or in an hour's time, you will have no idea. We do not plan our thoughts; they arise spontaneously.

One argument for this might be that our thoughts are always linked to our needs, drives, and desires. Therefore, I might start thinking about lunch because a feeling of hunger has arisen in my body. I might start thinking about going out to a club because of a sexual urge. And in a more complex way, I might think I need to do some study because I want to achieve good grades, which will get me a good job, which will secure me a steady income, so I don't have to worry about food and shelter in the future.

But the above explanations, which link thoughts to desires, fail to explain the often random nature of thought. Why does the theme tune to a TV show I haven't seen for years suddenly enter my mind while I am out taking a walk? Why, when asked to name any city in the world, do I choose Prague rather than Moscow?

It doesn't seem that we can argue that we are in control of our thoughts, so we must look for other reasons to explain why thoughts arise. I think there are only two possible explanations: either our thoughts must be determined by prior events, or they are being brought into existence by a power operating in the present moment, which is God.[1]

Creative thought is an obvious example of how thoughts are not determined by prior events. It would be absurd if the thoughts that a composer thinks while writing a symphony could be explained by evolution, or some kind of 'Big Bang' event, or childhood experiences. Seeing our present-moment thoughts as the result of the past simply doesn't make sense.

The random, unpredictable, and spontaneous nature of thought means that there is only one feasible explanation for why thoughts arise. There must be a power that is in control in the present moment, bringing our thoughts into and out of existence. That power is God.

Of course, it is not just thoughts that happen spontaneously. If we observe the unfolding of events within our consciousness, we can see that everything is happening spontaneously. Our hearts are beating spontaneously, our hair is growing spontaneously, we walk along without thinking how we walk, and we think without knowing how we think. The reason why all these things happen spontaneously is because God is doing them.

The fact that God is controlling our thoughts has very important implications for both philosophy and science. The philosophy of mind, for instance, is useless if it neglects God. Neuroscientists and other scientists have been examining the human brain for many years in order to try to understand thought. Their investigations are largely misguided because thought neither originates nor finds expression in the brain. It is people who think, rather than brains, and they do so by the power of God.

13

THE EXPERIENCE OF UNDERSTANDING

I have spent some time thinking about and examining the experience of understanding. In general, we are all able to relate to one another through conversation, whether spoken or written, and as you read these words you are most likely having the experience of understanding them. But why is this? What is the nature of this experience? Are the words that I type not merely a mishmash of lines and curly symbols on a page? At what point do they become meaningful and what is the cause of their meaning?

In this chapter, we'll briefly explore some answers to these questions.

Let's begin with a helpful quote from Bryan Magee which hones in on the problem.

If I listen to a sentence or a tune, the actual sensory input at any given instant can consist of no more than part of a single note, or pause, or consonant, or vowel sound. For me to hear the sentence *as a sentence*, or the tune *as a tune*, I need at each point in it to retain in my mind's ear all the sounds that have gone before, and to link them with one another and with my current aural input into something that I then apprehend as a whole.[1]

In the Western world of the twenty-first century, we are inclined to see cognition as a process carried out by our brains, which are often believed to be like machines or computers that process information and control our thoughts and actions. This is just one possibility I'd invite you to consider. Do you really feel as though there is a computer in your head powering your understanding, or does your understanding feel more organic and free-flowing than that?

Another possibility, and this is where I believe the truth of the matter rests, is that our experiences are brought about by God. God is behind every sensation, thought, and emotion that we experience. He is animating all of the processes that we experience as part of our aliveness; everything from our hearts beating, to our blinking, to our thinking — to our understanding. So, the reason why we experience the sensations associated with understanding a sentence or a tune is because God is giving us those experiences.

On close examination, what constitutes understanding is actually a series of subtle impressions in awareness that can be best described as sensations of tension and resolution. Tension is caused, I believe, when God makes us feel a degree of isolation, and resolution is a sense of greater connectedness with God's essence, which is love. Isolation and divine love are the two extremes of human experience, and the process of cognition is a subtle back-and-forth interplay between the two within our bodies.

But understanding also relates to objects, events, and ideas, rather than being merely bodily sensations. If this is true then it must be the case that God, who I believe is omniscient, is able to remember things. When I remember to pick up my keys before I leave the house, God has prompted that memory to arise in my awareness, so I believe it must be the case that God sees and comprehends the big picture, including all past events, and is able to produce in us thoughts and feelings that are related to the past.[2]

We must remember, though, that the past and future do not really exist. In reality, there is only an eternal now, which I believe contains the fullness of God. This moment, and God, are ultimately one and the same, and they constitute all that exists in reality. Therefore, it makes sense that God is in control of all our bodily processes, including the sensations and thoughts associated with the experience of under-standing.

14
_____

HEARING VOICES OR HEARING GOD?

Have you ever heard a Christian say, "God placed it on my heart" to do such and such? Let's take a brief look at what a statement like this might mean, and what it says about the relationship between God and human beings.

I believe that when we say God places something on our heart, what's really happening is that we are acknowledging that God is able to communicate directly with us. There is no chasm between God and human beings; on the contrary, God is intimately involved in all of our ideas, our motivations, and our desires.

This can only be the case if certain things are true about God. For instance, God must be present in our minds and in our bodies. This makes sense if we understand God to be omnipresent, as many theologians have proposed. Omnipresence means God is *literally* everywhere, including in every cell of our bodies.

In this context, is it so hard to imagine that God speaks to us?

I believe there is a certain stigma Christians feel about saying to unbelievers that God speaks to them, because they don't want to be judged as insane. To believers in God, it's quite a natural thing to say God spoke to us about this or that, but to unbelievers, who don't hear the voice of God, it can seem like a sign of mental illness.

The point I wish to make here is that it is perfectly normal, sane, and logical to experience God talking to us. I described this kind of experience in a post on my blog, part of which I have reproduced here:

> God is capable of producing in human beings a mode of mind that is like a veil – it prevents us being aware of Him. He is also able to reveal Himself to the human mind, by speaking directly to it in a mode similar to but distinct from

contemplative thought. It is God who makes thoughts arise in our minds, both contemplative thoughts, and those thoughts that are His speech to us. We can experience thoughts that are ours, and others that are God's. They are similar, but distinct, and all are from God.[1]

As you may recall from an earlier chapter, I like to refer to God as the 'cosmic animator', in control of all activity in the universe, which I refer to as His 'cosmic playground'. He is a living God, and He exists as boundless being in this single eternal moment. As I have already indicated, there is no separateness between God and any of His creation. It is therefore logical that as well as animating every-thing in the macrocosm (e.g. the movement of planets and other celestial objects), He is also animating everything in the microcosm (e.g. the beating of our hearts, the digestion of our food, the growing of our hair, and yes, even the workings of our minds).

There is a certain mystery about what exactly the mind is, but I believe neuroscientists are quite wrong when they use language that implies the mind is synonymous with the brain.[2] There is a spiritual dimension to thought, and I'm quite sure that thought has its origin in God, rather than in the physical matter of the brain.

I realise this understanding has profound implications for secular societies that hold to a materialist ideology. We seem to think that scanning brains holds the key to understanding the nature of thought and belief. Psychiatrists prescribe drugs that target the chemicals in our brains in order to try to counteract mental states that are seen as brain disorders. Perhaps the reason why there are so few recoveries from so-called mental illnesses is because they are treated in a materialistic rather than a spiritual way.[3]

God communicates with different people in different ways. Perhaps not every Christian hears the voice of God in the way I have described above, and that's perfectly okay. God is speaking to everyone all the time: when we read, when we converse, when we listen to music, and when we analyse, consider, and reflect. God also talks to people in more dramatic ways, like dreams and visions. But if God speaks directly to your mind in an intimate and personal way, it doesn't mean you are crazy; you are just in touch with the being who created you, who sustains you, and who animates your life.

Having explored the relationship between God and the human mind in some depth in Part 2, in Part 3 we will move on to the subject of religion — in particular, Christianity — and I will examine some of the fundamental doctrines of the Christian faith in light of my belief that God is unfolding all activity in existence.

PART III

CHRISTIANITY AND GOD

15

GOD'S GRAND GAME

My belief that God is the sustainer and animator of the whole of creation is somewhat controversial among Christians and others who believe in free will. After all, if we do not have free will, then ideas like sin, the fall, and judgment, don't necessarily make sense.

However, I believe there is a certain perspective (or a framework) in which these central Christian ideas can be understood in a different light, stemming from an understanding of God's true nature and what that means for His relationship with human beings. In this chapter, I will outline this framework.

. . .

God as Puppeteer

At the core of the framework is the idea that *whatever you do is what God is doing through you*. The best analogy I have found for this is that of a puppet show. In a puppet show, puppets can have distinct personalities and attributes and can be so realistic that a child who is watching the show might forget about the puppet master completely. We are puppets in the theatre of life and God is the puppeteer.

God's Omnipresence

In order for you to accept what I am saying about the way God is involved in creation, I ask you to consider His attribute of omnipresence. If God is omnipresent, there is no particle anywhere in creation which is not a part of Him. And it follows logically that everything that is a part of God must be under His control. So, if God is truly omnipresent, He is also in control of everything in existence.

Now although much of the time I am aware of God as I go about my daily life, because He speaks to me or because I feel His presence, at other times I am not directly aware of God, and it is during those times that I feel as though I am a free agent. As a person to whom God has revealed Himself, there are dimensions of my life in which I experience Him that can be particularly vivid — in prayer, or during a praise and worship session, for instance. At other times, while doing some chores around the house, working a job, or having a meal with friends, it's possible for me to be absorbed in these activities and lose that awareness.

But just because I lose my awareness of God in some situations doesn't mean He goes away. He is still omnipresent and in control of every aspect of my life, from my thoughts and words, to the functioning of my body and my every action. It simply means that there is a mode of mind that we experience as part of God's activity in our lives, where He makes us forget about Him. This is obviously an acute reality in the case of life-long atheists, who may never have an awareness of God, as He has totally veiled His existence in their minds and lives. It seems that God does not reveal Himself to everyone all of the time, and this is a central element of the game of human life that God is unfolding.

God's Control and the Christian Worldview

When we read the wonderful biblical narratives

depicting the interplay between God and His human creatures, we see that these stories reveal such inter-actions as command and obedience, action and judgment, prayer and response. In a world where God is omnipresent, this is peculiar, as in reality, God is in control of both the command and the obedience, the action of humans and subsequent judgment, and even their prayers and His response to their prayers. One can imagine a puppet praying to its puppet master to understand what I mean.

But let us consider this paradox in terms of the bigger picture concerning who God is. God is the extremely powerful, uncaused, necessarily existing, eternal being, who created the entire universe, and everything in it. He has all of eternity at His disposal. What will He do with all this power and all this time? It seems logical to me that He would create a complex universe — a cosmic playground — as a way of entertaining Himself as the vast aeons of eter-nity unfold.

What I propose is that God has created this great universe for His own pleasure, and unfolding the complex story of creation within the cosmic play-ground is God's pastime. In light of this, it makes sense that, as part of His grand game, God would create complex and wonderful story lines, such as those that we find in the Abrahamic religions (and other religions).

Conclusion

Within the framework that I have outlined in this chapter, Christianity makes sense, though not in a mainstream or traditional way. All of life is animated by God, so all the decisions a Christian makes — whether to obey Christ, whether to read the Bible, whether to visit their neighbour in hospital, whether to fast, repent, and believe — are the will of God in people's lives and are part of His grand game. The central events in the Christian story — the atoning sacrifice of Jesus Christ on the cross and His resurrection — are also part of God's storyline.

Believing as I do in an omnipresent God, this is the only way I can make sense of the Christian worldview. The fall is part of God's plan, and so is redemption. Sin is part of God's plan, and so is salvation. Atheism is part of God's plan, and so is faith.

This is not what most Christians believe, but without this framework, Christianity makes no sense at all, for I firmly believe that the cherished Christian idea of free will is not logically compatible with the idea that God is omnipresent. If you're going to accept the sovereignty of God over creation, you must also accept that we don't have free will,[1] and so a framework such as the one outlined in this chapter becomes a necessary way of making sense of the Christian worldview.

16

IS JESUS THE ONLY WAY?

I spent many years as a Christian. During times when I have been immersed in Christian life and enthusiastically proclaiming the gospel message, there has been an urgency to my endeavours owing to a passion for Jesus and a fear that everyone who isn't saved is going to hell. This is the basis for Christian evangelism, and this is why Christian evangelists can often seem pushy; they genuinely feel they have an exclusive claim to truth, and that the only way to avoid eternal punishment is by becoming a believer.

But if God is the omnipresent creator of the universe, then He has created every religion, not just Christianity. He is the creator of millions of

Muslims, Jews, Mormons, Sikhs, and Jehovah's Witnesses. He is also the creator of all those people who are atheists, or agnostics. He has created literally billions of people who have lived and died outside of the Christian faith. Can it really be the case that all of these lives, with all their richness and diversity, are meaningless because they are empty of Jesus Christ?

An alternative view would be that creation is a rich tapestry in which every thread, or every person, has a distinct and meaningful role to play. Existence can be seen as a grand performance in which God is expressing His infinite power by creating great diversity. Everyone who has lived and died has played out their role in God's grand game, and God will bring everything together in a coherent way in the future.

Some Christians argue that nonbelievers are judged 'by the light they have received', meaning that even if they haven't heard the gospel, they are still morally culpable, as they have been exposed to good and evil and have had to choose accordingly. This is a way of accommodating all those outside of the faith into the Christian worldview.

But I wonder whether every life might be valuable to

God in its own right, because if God is the sovereign creator, sustainer, and animator of all there is, then each individual's life has unfolded in exactly the way God intended, even if they did not embrace Jesus as Lord and Saviour and live a Christian life.

17

THE MYTH OF THE FALL

A major idea in the Christian tradition is that human beings live in a 'fallen' state. The idea is that, through original sin (which took place in the Garden of Eden), humanity fell from its original state of union with God, which had been experienced by Adam and Eve before they made the decision to eat the 'forbidden fruit' from the Tree of Knowledge of Good and Evil. This decision corrupted their nature and brought sin into the world. Christians believe that we all inherit a sinful nature, or separation from God, due to the actions of that first created man, Adam, when he ate the forbidden fruit in the Garden of Eden. Many believe that the serpent in the story, who tempts Eve to take the forbidden fruit, is the devil (also referred to by Christians as

Satan/Lucifer), an angel which has itself fallen from God.

There is no doubt that this story has mythical qualities, even if many Christians do believe it to be literally true. For our purposes, we are concerned with the relationship between God and man, and whether or not there has been a fall away from God, as the story suggests.

It is difficult for me to understand how anything can exist in a state of separation from God. What is it that creates, sustains, moves, and animates the world, if not God? Would a tree really know how to grow itself, without God being the active agent that grows the tree? I cannot understand how this would be so. To take a human example, how is it that a person could possibly know how to beat their heart, flow their blood, grow their hair and nails, digest food, or any of the other processes that we experience as part of our living state, without God being the doer of these actions?

It seems to me that the idea of a fall is illogical, because God is clearly in control of everything that happens.

Time and time again, Christians come up against the contradictions inherent in their belief in free will. I have heard Christians say that God is responsible for them finding a great church, or giving them a baby, or a new job. But those same Christians maintain that it is their human free will that chooses to sin: to walk away from church, to abuse their baby, or to lie about their job. It is surely obvious that Christians are disastrously unclear about what is God's action in the world, and what is free human action. I have never known a Christian to be able to speak coherently about the things that God is doing, as opposed to the things that humans are doing.

The problem with the Christian worldview is that free will is ascribed to human beings when, in reality, we cannot possibly be free. If God is omnipresent, as many theologians agree He is, then God must be responsible for *all* action and not *some* action. Everything that happens must be the result of God acting in the world.

There never was a fall away from God, and there never can be.

A much more sensible approach to theology is to realise that God is necessarily everywhere and in everything. Once we admit this truth, we can then start to form a worldview and a theology that is logical, because it relates to reality, rather than to a myth that cannot make sense of the way the world really is.

18

THE CONFUSION OF CALVINISM

I am subscribed to the *Desiring God* mailing list[1] and often read the words of John Piper, who answers questions about Christian doctrine from curious believers.

Through the mailing list I became aware of an article on Piper's website entitled "Does God Control All Things All the Time?".[2] I was excited to discover Piper had written on this subject, as it's an area of particular philosophical interest to me. I was genuinely intrigued to read what Piper had to say about this question, which cuts into the heart of Christian theology.

As I read through the article, I found myself in almost total agreement. For instance, I agree that

God works all things out according to His will, that God governs all human plans and acts, and that anything that Satan does must ultimately be under God's control. I tend to agree with a lot of what Calvinists like Piper have to say about God's sovereignty. But just as Piper was concluding his response to the question, he made a statement that I think highlights why I could not ultimately describe myself as a Calvinist:

> God's sovereignty does not diminish our accountability.

Alarm bells immediately started ringing in my mind and my heart sank as I read these words, which represent a confusion that is at the heart of Calvinist thinking. Earlier in the article, Piper had made another statement along the same lines:

> Even in situations where God is permitting, He is permitting by design.

Are you able to see the contradiction that exists in these two statements? You see, Calvinists want to strongly state God's sovereignty and do so by insisting that salvation is solely a work of God. But the trouble is we only need to be 'saved' because of rebellion against God, and this rebellion implies freedom of the human will. *Without God's sovereignty, Calvinism doesn't make sense, but with God's sovereignty, Christianity doesn't make sense.*

It's simple. If we are free to sin, then God is not in control of our lives, and so we cannot call Him sovereign. If we are not free to sin, and our lives are under God's control, then the need for salvation, and therefore the whole Christian gospel, evaporates.

Calvinists would have to deny what I affirm, which is that we are merely puppets in the hands of God. I believe all of creation is part of God — He is omnipresent — and this is what true divine sovereignty means. We have to be able to affirm this truth about God and then deal with the implications for our theology, which are far-reaching, and which I have discussed at length in my essay entitled "An Almighty Predicament: A Discourse on the Arguments For and Against Christianity".[3]

Reformed Christian thinkers with a high view of God's sovereignty will often try to sneak in free will through the metaphorical back door by arguing that, prior to salvation, we are 'dead in our sins' and under the 'bondage of the will'. Such phrases are a veiled attempt to deny God is in control of our sins, and Calvinists cling to such phrases because, as I have argued above, the Christian worldview doesn't make sense if He is *wholly* in control. The truth of the matter is that we are not so much slaves to *sin* as slaves to *God*, who controls every aspect of our lives, from our very conception and including those aspects of our behaviour that Christians might describe as sinful.

19

MOLINISM REFUTED

A theological position that has risen to prominence in recent years is that of Molinism. Getting its name from the sixteenth-century Jesuit theologian Luis de Molina, but brought to prominence in our time by the American debater William Lane Craig, the position attempts to reconcile God's sovereignty with human free will.

Anyone who has read much of my writing will know that this subject is one I believe is at the heart of Christian theology, and theology in general. In this chapter, I will explain the central tenets of Molinism, and will suggest that while it may be a philosophically interesting theory, when we relate the theory to the real world, it actually makes no sense at all.

Molina's theory is a complex one, but I will give a brief explanation.

Molina posits that God has three different types of knowledge: natural knowledge, free knowledge, and middle knowledge. Natural knowledge is God's knowledge of all logical possibilities, that is to say, everything that is necessarily true. An example of one such truth is 'all bachelors are unmarried'. God's free knowledge refers to everything that God has 'actualised', that is, the knowledge of everything He has freely created. And finally, between these two types of knowledge is middle knowledge, which includes anything that would happen in a certain set of circumstances.

At the outset I should say I find these definitions of God's knowledge to be problematic as they appear to turn God into a kind of 'logic machine', where He is limited by the rules of logic as though they exist in some kind of Platonic ideal realm. This is not the way I believe God to be at all. I believe God is much simpler than the Molinist position implies. Nevertheless, let us consider the theory.

For our purposes, we will focus on 'middle knowledge', the aspect of Molina's theological perspective that has been considered to hold the answer to the divine sovereignty versus human free will predicament.

In a video entitled "What is Molinism?", Craig explains the position:

> What Molina said is that logically prior to God's creating the world, God knew what any free creature that He might create would freely do in any set of circumstances in which He might place that person.[1]

This is so-called 'middle knowledge', which Craig defines elsewhere as follows:

> Middle knowledge is God's knowledge of what people would do freely in any set of circumstances, and those people may never exist.[2]

So, as I understand the position, Molinists believe that, prior to creation, there are an infinite number of possible worlds, all of which God knows everything about. Within those worlds, God knows every choice that any free person would make in any set of circumstances (and this is true before He has even decided to create a person). God picks one of these possible worlds to be the actual world and thereby puts each person in a set of circumstances that He is perfectly in control of, so He knows exactly what they will do, but they are still free to act in whichever way they choose.

To even conceptualise this is a real struggle, but as I mentioned above, it's a complicated theory. I am confident, however, that I am able to grasp enough of the theory to see why it fails. So, I will now offer three refutations in response to the theory, all of which are interrelated.

1. *It is impossible for anyone to do anything freely.* God, by His very nature, is omnipresent, which means that there are no boundaries to God's being. If God has no boundaries, it logically follows that every atom in existence is a part of God and therefore under God's control. In this context, free will is impossible.

2. *There is no separation between God and man.* Molinism says that we have man on the one hand (who is free), and man's circumstances on the other hand (determined by God). But in reality, it is

impossible to draw a distinction between man and his circumstances because there is no dividing line in terms of where one ends and the other begins. For instance, is your breathing caused by you or your circumstances? How about your choice of clothes or food? If you consider the answers to these questions, it should be obvious that you cannot separate man and his circumstances into two separate categories. Really, all that exists is a single present moment unfolding that is not ontologically distinct from God. Entities within this unfolding are merely aspects or appearances of God, and crucially, that includes human beings.

3. *Creation is an ongoing process.* Craig's view of the universe is that it was created at a specific point in time long ago (in a 'Big Bang' event). But if this is the case, what is God doing right now? The separation between God and creation is a fiction; creation didn't happen at a specific point in the past, but on the contrary, God is unfolding all events right now in the present moment. The past and future, which are necessary components of Craig's take on Molinism, don't exist in reality; they are just ideas in the minds of creatures.

If we deeply consider the nature of God, it is easy to

see why Molinism fails to reconcile the divine sovereignty versus human free will predicament. The solution to that predicament is the realisation that all that exists does so within God, and is therefore under God's control. There is no free will, and once we realise this, the need to posit God's 'middle knowledge', as Molina and Craig have done, evaporates.

20

JESUS THE CREATOR?

The idea that anything has existed eternally is mind boggling. But, as I contemplate the oneness of God from a panentheistic perspective (the belief that everything exists 'in God'), I can almost make sense of the idea. I am much more comfortable with the idea that one thing (being, essence) has always existed than that multiple things have always existed.

But Christian apologists often argue that Jesus and the Holy Spirit have existed eternally along with God the Father. This seems to indicate that Jesus, the God-man who walked the earth two thousand years ago, is somehow uncreated. This is a difficult idea to understand, so let's look at a few of the key scriptures that give Christians confidence in Jesus' eternal nature.

John the Evangelist quotes Jesus as saying,

> And now, Father, glorify me in your presence with the glory I had with you before the world began. (John 17:5 NIV)

The apostle Paul, in his letter to the church in Corinth, explains,

> yet for us there is but one God, the Father, from whom all things came and for whom we live; and there is but one Lord, Jesus Christ, through whom all things came and through whom we live. (1 Corinthians 8:6 NIV)

And in his letter to the Colossians, Paul further elaborates:

> The Son is the image of the invisible God, the firstborn over all creation. For in him all things were created: things in heaven and on earth, visible and invisible, whether thrones or powers or rulers or authorities; all things have been

created through him and for him. He is before all things, and in him all things hold together. (Colossians 1:15-17 NIV)

When we consider the above scriptures, I think there is an important point that needs to be made. To say Jesus existed eternally is different from saying Jesus existed before the world began. It could be the case, for instance, that God has created other worlds and other universes before the one in which we live, where there may have been no human beings and no Jesus Christ. Let us not forget that eternity is a very, very, long time, and it is quite possible that the revelation we have received in the Bible is for our world, and not every world and every creation that God has ever brought forth.

Perhaps Jesus was created before the world, and everything was indeed created through Him as the above scriptures suggest. I realise that this idea conflicts somewhat with the concept of an uncreated eternal Trinity, but as I have already mentioned, I find it much easier to believe that God existed as one before He existed as three persons. I realise that this is to say that Jesus was *created* before He became *creator* of our present world.

When I think about the idea of Jesus existing eternally, the picture I have in my mind is of a *human being* existing eternally. But before the incarnation, did Jesus exist in some other form? Was Jesus a spiritual entity without a human form (e.g. the 'word' or 'logos' of John 1)? If so, how are we to understand Jesus' form at that time? I'm not sure the Bible tells us the answer to this question, but perhaps I am mistaken.

The intention of this chapter is merely to encourage readers to think deeply about the common Christian claim that Jesus has existed for as long as God the Father. Is it possible for a *complex* creator — comprised of multiple entities — to have eternal existence? Or must an eternal being necessarily be *simple*, and only one? Personally, I find the latter view of God to be far more intellectually satisfactory.

21

THE AUTHORITY OF SCRIPTURE

The question of authority in matters of faith is important for any believer in God to consider. Within Christianity specifically, there is heated debate as to whether the Bible is a sufficient authority in all spiritual matters, as many theologians who advocate for *sola scriptura* believe.[1] A contrary position would be that God has given authority in spiritual matters to human beings (the Pope being the obvious example), as Catholics believe.

In this chapter we will examine what it means to say Scripture holds authority and I will present the reasons why I believe it is problematic to argue that the Bible is in itself authoritative.

In the book *Scripture Alone* by American Christian apologist James White, there is a paragraph that I believe encapsulates the predicament very well:

> [W]ithout the highest view of Scripture, we can never claim to have heard God with certainty, and hence we cannot teach and preach with any more authority than that which we can create for ourselves.[2]

While I understand the argument being made here, I think it raises questions about the way in which God communicates with human beings through Scripture. For instance, what about the issue of interpretation? Isn't the one who interprets Scripture by that very activity becoming an authority in respect of what that Scripture says?

It is an undeniable truth that there are contradictions in views on doctrinal issues among Christians who share a high view of Scripture. Can it ever be the case that one particular reading of Scripture reflects what is absolutely true? Are some readings right and some wrong, or are different perspectives equally valid? How are we to know?

When considering the authority of Scripture within

the Christian faith, we should not neglect to think about the deep issue of how meaning and interpretation work on an epistemological level.[3]

Whenever we read anything (Scripture or otherwise), God is working in our bodies and minds to bring about understanding. The words we read are merely markings on a page; there is no inherent meaning in these symbols, as if somehow the markings contained ideas within their ink, or could interpret themselves.[4] No, understanding is a work of God, who uses His infinite knowledge to illumine our finite minds as we read and reflect.

I believe this work of God is not solely limited to people of a particular faith — God, as cosmic animator, is at work in every human being, directing the activity of our minds and all of our thoughts, words, and actions as we read and reflect, regardless of which text we happen to be reading.

To single out the Christian Scriptures as the only written revelation God has given to humanity can be seen to be illogical, as He is clearly controlling interpretation in every situation where words are being read and understood. After all, God is not just sovereign over the lives of Reformed Christians, but over the lives of all human beings.

This is not to deny that God might use the Bible to talk to Christians in a unique way. There are certainly modes of mind that I experienced as a Christian that were related to the particular churches with which I was involved, and the particular interpretations of Scripture which they supported. But it is also true that God uses other texts to communicate with other groups of people in different ways, and this should be understood and not denied.

Seeing the matter of interpretation in this light allows us to offer a much more inclusive vision of God than Reformed theology allows, as we can logically infer that God speaks to people of different faith groups through their own holy scriptures, as well as to the secular individual who is reading a novel, for example. The *sola scriptura* advocate may argue that this hermeneutic is a recipe for moral anarchy, for if we do not have the moral instruction contained (they would argue) within the Bible, how are we to know what is right and wrong? The answer to this question is discussed in Part 5 ("Morality and God").

Elevating the importance of the Bible to the exclusion of other books can be dangerous, as what is really happening is that the one interpreting the Bible is becoming 'a law unto himself', imposing his interpretation on all who are prepared to listen. Of course, God is involved in this process, and leaders within the Christian church will point out that God has given them their position of authority and leadership. I agree that He has, but in the same way that He has raised up authorities within the church, He has also raised up authorities in other faith groups, and in the secular world. To argue that God is in control of the vocations of Christian leaders but not other faith leaders would be highly illogical, and would stem from a misunderstanding concerning the nature of God and specifically His sovereignty over all events.

When a Christian who advocates for *sola scriptura* relaxes their high view of the Bible, their sense of personal authority may diminish, but this could be a positive thing as it will allow them to be more open-minded and inclusive of other perspectives and the way in which God speaks through other books to other people.

22

WHAT PRAYER REVEALS ABOUT GOD

Implicit within prayer is the acknowledgment that God is in control of our lives. If it were not the case that God is in control, it wouldn't make sense to pray to Him.

In this chapter, I will give a few examples of how Christians trust in God's omnipotence and omnipresence when they pray. I will explain why such beliefs, while demonstrating the believer's trust in God's power, simultaneously create problems for the Christian worldview.

God is in control of our relationships. For instance, Christians pray to meet a future spouse, or pray for God to grow and bless their friendships, or their marriage.

God is in control of our circumstances. Christians would naturally pray for God to bless them with a new job. They might pray that God would bless their friends or relatives with a safe journey, indicating God is in control of all circumstances related to transport. Christians often pray for God to plant them in a great church, or to help them pass an exam.

God is in control of the weather. Christians pray for rain for our crops, or for severe weather to be calmed, or for a bright and sunny wedding day.

God is in control of our bodies. Christians pray to be healed of sicknesses and diseases.

God is in control of society. Christians pray for God to raise up good leaders in our political parties, and for Him to protect and bless our countries. Christians regularly pray for God to bless those who are living in poverty, or for those who are being persecuted.

God is in control of evil. Christians pray for God to deliver them from evil (for instance, by reciting the Lord's Prayer), and to protect them from the schemes of the devil, or from the wickedness of their enemies.

My argument, then, is that Christians know that God is in control of everything that happens, and this is reflected in the way they pray to God. But if God is in control of everything that happens, this necessarily implies there is no free will. Therefore, central Christian doctrines such as sin, judgment, salvation, and the fall of man, don't make sense.[1]

In Part 3, we have explored some of the key ideas at the heart of the Christian faith, and criticised them in relation to my argument that we do not have free will. We will now proceed to consider the free will problem from a range of different angles, in order that I may solidify my argument that all events in existence — that is, God's cosmic playground — are willed and directed by God and are part of the grand game He is unfolding.

PART IV

FREE WILL

23

MATERIALISM AND FREE WILL

Over the last few years, the American philosopher Sam Harris has received a great deal of recognition among atheists, who see him as an important figure, championing science as pitted against religion when it comes to the subject of morality.

Having spent many hours watching videos of Harris speaking and debating with various scholarly opponents, I appreciate that he is a sharp and articulate thinker with some good insights. I do, however, believe that his approach to morality and, in particular, free will is flawed in a significant way. I would like to make a few simple but crucial points in response to Harris's book entitled *Free Will*.[1]

Harris is right to point out that we don't have free

will. Like Harris, I have taken the time to examine this subject in depth, both by reading widely on the subject and by examining my own subjective experience. Harris points out that our thoughts arise spontaneously and that we have no control over them, which is something I have also noted in my written works.[2] As I wrote in the earlier chapter entitled "What is Causing Our Thoughts?", we have no idea what we will be thinking in a minute's time, or an hour's time. *We do not control our thoughts; they arise spontaneously.*

Harris, who has studied neuroscience, resolves this problem in a materialistic way. He believes that what comprises a person is merely physical. He states, for example, that if every atom in his body were exchanged with those of someone else, he would become that person. This materialistic outlook causes Harris to place undue importance on the brain as the primary cause of human experience.

In his own words, Harris explains:

> There is no question that (most, if not all) mental events are the product of physical events. The brain is a physical system, entirely beholden to the laws of nature – and there is every reason to

believe that changes in its functional state and material structure entirely dictate our thoughts and actions.[3]

The flaw in this thinking is that it ignores the spiritual aspect of reality. If there is a God who animates all activity in existence, as I have argued throughout this book, then it is God who is causing thoughts to arise in our minds, as well as controlling all our bodily processes, such as our heartbeat, digestion, and circulation.

How something that is purely material could create awareness of the kind that human beings experience is an area of ceaseless confusion for neuroscientists. Many attempt to resolve the problem by appealing to the 'subconscious', a mysterious entity which is often referred to by scientists and psychological therapists, but that no one is able to understand or define in any meaningful way. In reality, I believe the need to posit 'unconscious causes',[4] as Harris does, can be dispensed with when we understand that God is in control of all our experiences.

A concise summary of the fallacy believed by many neuroscientists is encapsulated in the following quote from Harris:

> Although we notice changes in our experience –
> in thought, mood, perception, behaviour, etc. –
> we are utterly unaware of the neurophysiological
> events that produce them.[5]

Such an assertion — that our experience is somehow caused by neurophysiological events — stems from a false assumption about the role of the brain. If the brain is somehow in control of our experiences, one would have to ask what is in control of the brain, and this is something I believe neuroscience fails to address, but my own philosophy does.[6]

Rather than being the mere output of an evolutionary process (combined with our life circumstances) as Harris maintains, the truth is that *we are puppets in the hands of a living God*, and He is directing all the physical and immaterial aspects of our existence. God is alive right now in this single eternal moment, and everything is unfolding by His sovereign will.

My description of God as the cosmic animator will make sense only to those who have deeply examined the nature of thought and consciousness or to those whom God has spoken or revealed Himself in other ways. There are many solid arguments for the existence of God, as I have expounded in the earlier chapter "How Do I Know God Exists?", but knowing God always depends upon some kind of revelation.

If we consider the nature of God, particularly His attribute of omnipresence, it makes sense that He is controlling our conscious experiences because His being permeates every atom in existence and every cell of our bodies.

There are, of course, moral implications to this worldview, which I believe Harris (if he were to accept my worldview) would acknowledge and understand. He speaks intelligently about the subject of culpability in the criminal justice system, and makes the important point that we can look with a greater sense of empathy and understanding upon criminal behaviour when we appreciate we don't have free will. I completely agree, but, in my view, it is God who is in control rather than the blind forces of evolution and circumstance.

I do realise, of course, that the God I'm depicting is not the God that most Christians, Muslims, or Jews embrace. Indeed, it is central to these religions that we have free will and are responsible for sin and deserving of judgment. My perspective calls into question our accountability, as it makes God the author of everything that might be described as 'sin' or 'evil'. This can be a hard idea for theists to fathom, but I believe it is the truth, and I have discussed it at length in Part 5.

In the human dimension of reality, we experience the illusion of free will, but this is merely a mode of mind under God's control.[7] In the ultimate dimension of reality, God is responsible for our every thought, word, and deed.[8]

It is liberating to have discovered that God is in control of everything in existence, both in the microcosm and the macrocosm. This discovery solves many of the problems that neuroscientists are wrestling with, by dispensing with the false idea that our experiences are caused by unconscious neurological events.

Sam Harris has correctly deduced that we don't have free will, and this truth, should it become widely accepted, will have profound implications for the moral issues of our time. But as we consider the way society deals with moral issues, we need to shift our focus away from neuroscience and onto the theological matter of God's relationship with human beings, as it is the timeless truth of God's existence, and more specifically His omnipresence, that holds the key to correctly understanding why free will is ultimately an illusion.

24

THE BIBLE AND FREE WILL

For some time now, I have been arguing that God is in control of all activity in existence, both on the human level and in the world at large. I would like to present a series of biblical scriptures that support this worldview, all the while acknowledging that there are other scriptures that may be interpreted to reflect different views of the relationship between God and His creation.

As I explained in the chapter entitled "The Authority of Scripture," I believe all Scripture is subject to any particular interpretations that God brings to our minds as we read and reflect. Meaning is not intrinsic within a text. However, as I make my arguments in this chapter and throughout this book,

I trust that God, if He is willing, will use my words to communicate truths and insights to the minds of readers.

I don't believe in the devil as a free, autonomous being. This is because I believe that God's literal omnipresence leaves no room for free will, an argument that I make emphatically throughout this book. Everything that exists, including the devil (if he exists, which is debatable), is part of God and therefore under God's control. I reach out to God in prayer in the knowledge that He really is in control of everything that happens. Below are a few scriptures from the Bible which support this position.

> I form the light and create darkness, I bring prosperity and create disaster; I, the Lord, do all these things. (Isaiah 45:7 NIV)

Many Christians believe the devil is in control of all that we consider to be evil in the world. The passage from Isaiah clearly demonstrates that it is God who creates 'disaster' in the world and not the devil.

> Who can speak and have it happen, if the Lord has not decreed it? Is it not from the mouth of the

Most High that both calamities and good things come? (Lamentations 3:37-38 NIV)

Once again, this passage makes it clear that God is in control of all those things in life that we would consider to be calamities. Surely, we must conclude either that God is in control of those things that we consider 'evil', or the rebellious Satan is in control of such calamities. The above scripture demonstrates it is God who is in control.

I know that you can do all things, and that no purpose of yours can be thwarted. (Job 42:2 NIV)

This passage, in which Job speaks directly to God, clearly demonstrates God's sovereign power over all events. The implication here is that no purpose of God's can be thwarted because He is in control of all things and therefore all events. This could not be the case if Satan was in control of certain purposes.

Remember the former things of old; for I am God, and there is no other; I am God, and there is none like me, declaring the end from the beginning and from ancient times things not yet done, saying 'My counsel shall stand, and I will accomplish all my purpose' (Isaiah 46:9-10 ESV)

God clearly has the power to accomplish any purpose which He wills. This would not be the case if there was a being in opposition to Him (the devil) that had power to act against His sovereign will.

The Lord has made everything for its purpose, even the wicked for the day of trouble. (Proverbs 16:4 ESV)

It couldn't be any clearer that God is in control of both those things that we consider 'good' and those things which we consider 'evil'. God is omnipotent and omnipresent and is therefore in control of everything that happens.

We may find it hard to understand why God creates things that we consider to be evil, as well as things that we consider to be good.[1] But just because it is a difficult problem to respond to does not mean we should deny the reality that we see exemplified here in Scripture. It may well be the case that there is a being called the devil in existence. But these scriptures demonstrate that this being, if he exists, is under God's control, and so we would have to say that ultimately God is responsible for his actions.

Christians believe that God is working all things together for good for those who trust in Him and are called according to His purpose (Romans 8:28), and I believe we should always see evil in the light that God ultimately brings good out of the bad. But this shouldn't lead us to deny that God, as our creator and sustainer, is and always has been in control of *all* things, both 'good' and 'evil'.

25

COMPATIBILISM

In this chapter, I want to look at the idea of compatibilism as discussed by the theologian D. A. Carson in a book entitled *Still Sovereign*.[1] The book features fourteen essays by Calvinist scholars on a range of theological subjects. The chapter by Carson I'll be responding to here is entitled "Reflections on Assurance," but while the chapter as a whole discusses how Christians can have assurance of their salvation, I want to focus on just a few paragraphs on the subject of compatibilism.

Let's start with Carson's definition of compatibilism:

Compatibilism is the view that the following two statements are, despite superficial evidence to the contrary, mutually compatible: God is absolutely sovereign but his sovereignty does not in any way mitigate human responsibility; human beings are responsible creatures (i.e., they choose, decide, obey, disobey, believe, rebel, and so forth), but their responsibility never serves to make God absolutely contingent.[2]

Christians of the Reformed tradition tend to believe that the Bible is the ultimate authority on all theological matters, so Carson naturally seeks to explore what the Bible says about compatibilism. He writes, "My contention is that the biblical writers, insofar as they reveal themselves on this subject, are without exception compatibilists."[3]

Carson proceeds to give a few examples of biblical passages that demonstrate this assertion, including the obvious example of Genesis 50:19-20, where Joseph is sold into slavery by his brothers and the scripture says they meant it for evil, while God meant it for good (Joseph ends up in very blessed circumstances). The idea here is that the brothers' actions were undertaken of their own free will, but, at the same time, were a part of God's plan for Joseph's life.

In the New Testament, Carson sees evidence of compatibilism even in the event at the heart of Christianity: Christ's death on the cross. The crucifixion of Jesus, Carson explains, is surely part of God's plan for humanity, but that doesn't excuse the actions of the "human players" such as Herod, Judas, Pontius Pilate, and so on.

Carson then makes the important point that if humans do not have responsibility, what would be the point of Christ dying for our sins, as surely there would be no guilt if God causes sin to happen? Why the necessity for an atoning sacrifice?

The centrality and vital importance of this discussion is summed up by Carson.

> I have no idea how to conceptualize a God who is both sovereign and personal, but I perceive that if both are not simultaneously true, the God of the Bible disappears, and Christianity, indeed theism itself, is destroyed. In short, the mystery of compatibilism is traceable to the mystery of God, to what we do not know about God.[4]

The ideas expressed in this quotation have huge implications. What Carson is saying is that, because it is so central to the Bible, if we don't accept compatibilism, then Christianity doesn't make sense. But at the same time the author explains that compatibilism is a mystery of God, implying that we can't really make sense of the idea.

It seems to me, then, that if we are living by reason, we reject compatibilism as an illogical concept. I have argued throughout this book that God is omnipresent and in control of everything that happens and, because of that, we do not have free will. To me that is logical and incidentally solves the compatibilist problem.

But if the Bible teaches compatibilism, and the Bible is God's revelation to mankind, should we suspend logic and reason and live purely by faith in what we read in the Scriptures? Is it really possible to commit our lives to a belief that in a significant way, doesn't make sense? I invite readers to consider this predicament which, for me, poses a significant problem for the Christian worldview.[5]

26

OPEN THEISM

In this chapter, I will try to explain in a concise and simple way some of the main elements of the theological movement known as Open Theism. Most of my knowledge on this subject comes from internet articles and online video debates featuring leading theologians in this field. I will aim to represent the tenets of Open Theism accurately and will offer some criticisms of Openist theology based on my own beliefs about free will and the nature of God.

Open Theists (or 'Openists') use Scripture to illustrate the idea that God can change His mind. For instance, I have heard Openists cite the biblical passage 2 Kings 20: 1-4 to illustrate this. In this passage, God tells Hezekiah to get his house in order as he is going to die. Hezekiah protests and pleads with God, and in response God agrees to let him live for another fifteen years.

The question here is whether God had decreed these events from eternity past (as Calvinists would claim), or whether God was responding to Hezekiah within time at the moment he pleaded. Openists assert that we have free will, and therefore that God can change His mind in response to actions freely undertaken by human beings.

I would have to take issue with the Openist position on the grounds that I do not believe human beings have free will. As I have tried to make clear throughout this book, omnipresence is an attribute of God, and this being so, He is in control of all action in existence. God would have been in control of every aspect of Hezekiah's life, including his illness, his pleading, and his subsequent recovery following the apparent change of mind from God.

What we need to understand is that God did not create the universe and then sit back and watch it unfold in an automatic way, but rather He actively animates the universe and all its parts in this single eternal present moment. God is living. *There is no atom in existence which is not under the direct control of God.* So, when we read this biblical story about God changing His mind, we have to remember that Hezekiah is just a puppet in God's grand plan, which He unfolds in accordance with His divine will as the centuries go by.

Existence, I believe, is like a game. In Hinduism, there is a term called 'lila' which doesn't really have a parallel in English, but loosely describes life as God's 'play'. God is glorifying Himself through His creation and He is the sole agent that creates, sustains, and acts, in order to express some of the infinite possibilities that are contained within His nature.

Throughout the Bible, events are presented as though human beings have free will to which God responds. I believe this free will is illusory. There is a certain mode of mind that human beings experience, which is like a veil that can prevent us from being aware of God, but this veil is part of the way God has created humans to be. God reveals Himself to some people during our earthly lives (we could say He 'lifts the veil'), and to others He remains veiled; this is all part of the 'lila' and God's plan for mankind.

I believe we need to understand the Bible and the Hezekiah story in this context. The 'play' that goes on between God and Hezekiah is completely within God's control, and all of the many instances where there is rebellion against God in the Bible are also part of this divine play.

Keeping all of this in mind, let us look at a few other features of Open Theism. In a 2015 video entitled "Greg Boyd on open theism (the open view of the future),"[1] using scriptural references to back up his position, Openist Greg Boyd asserts the following things about God:

God regrets (Genesis 6:6-7)

God confronts improbabilities (Isaiah 5:1-5)

God gets frustrated (Ezekiel 22:30-31)

God tests people (e.g. Abraham in Genesis 22:12)

God speaks of the future using subjunctive terms, e.g. 'if' or 'may' (Exodus 13:17)

All of the above statements are intended to defend the view that God's will changes as time unfolds. I would agree with the idea that God can change His mind, for He is all-powerful and sovereign and in control of everything that happens. Why shouldn't He make changes to His plans at any time if He wills to do so?

The Openist belief in free will raises the further question of how the will of God and the will of humans interact. It is important to ask, 'What is God doing, and what are humans doing?'. If you have never considered this problem in depth before, I'll suggest a simple exercise you might undertake. Simply divide a blank document into two columns, and on the left list the things that you believe man does freely, and on the right list those things which you believe God is controlling. This simple exercise should be sufficient to make you think deeply about the problem, and to realise that there is no dividing line between God's activity and human activity.

To me, it is obvious that God is sustaining me in every moment; He is flowing my blood, beating my heart, blinking my eyelids, controlling my breath, digesting food in my stomach, bringing thoughts to my mind, and yes, even typing these words through me. He is also working in your body and mind as you read, converting markings on a page into meaningful impressions in your mind. If you consider this deeply, isn't it obvious that God is making you be? Can you see that He is in control?

We do not have free will.

For the Openist, the future is not eternally settled, but is at least partly open to possibilities. God knows all things, including the past, the present, and some of the future. God knows all possibilities, but we still have freedom. God is both stable and flexible. God is stable in every respect in which it is virtuous to be stable, but God is flexible in every respect in which it is virtuous to be flexible. The idea here is that free will is a gift given to us by God in order that we may choose to enter into a loving relationship with Him.

This perspective allows the Openist to maintain that God is perfectly loving, in contrast with a Calvinistic worldview, for instance, in which God is in control of suffering. My own view, of course, is that God is indeed in control of all suffering, but Calvinists affirm we do have free will (albeit a will in bondage to sin) which, as I have explained in the chapter entitled "The Confusion of Calvinism," is why I'm not a Calvinist.

The Openist view is that, in any given moment, the future consists of many possibilities. God is infinitely wise and therefore knows every possibility. My problem here is that Openists seem to divide all activity into events, and seemingly a finite number of possible events. It would be difficult for anyone to assert that God knows infinite possible courses of action in every possible situation, as that gives us infinite infinities, which is a concept that doesn't really make sense, even if God is omnipotent. In reality, of course, there are no separate events, as so-called events flow into one another. There is really only one eternal event without beginning or end — the eternal now, which is not ontologically distinct from God.

In summary, then, the Openists defend a belief in human free will and say that God changes His mind in response to human action. There are clearly scriptures that can be used to support such a belief, but I believe this perspective fails to take into account the true nature of God as omnipresent and therefore as being in control of all so-called 'events'.

27

DIVINE CONSERVATION AND OCCASIONALISM

I have studied Philosophy and Religion at postgraduate level but it is rare that I come across views of philosophers and theologians that resonate with my own beliefs about the God/world relationship. So, I was pleased to stumble upon some articles expressing two philosophical ideas that I can relate to. The two ideas — Divine Conservation and Occasionalism — may sound rather cumbersome and dull, but I believe they are interesting and important. In this chapter, I wish to explain these two ideas as simply as I can and explain why they are important and how they relate to my own philosophical outlook.

· · ·

The Doctrine of Divine Conservation

Let us start with a definition of the Doctrine of Divine Conservation:

> In Western monotheism, especially the monotheisms of the Abrahamic tradition, God is conceived to be both the creator and sustainer of all that exists. Such a conception yields doctrines of creation and conservation, where the first concerns the origin of things and the second the continued existence of things.[1]

What we are examining here is what holds objects in existence. Deists argue that God created the world but does not play an active role in sustaining it. They might say that the rules of physics are sufficient to explain why matter exists, and that there is no necessity to speculate that God is holding anything in existence.

Those who believe in Divine Conservation would take an opposing view; God is not only the creator of matter but also the sustainer (or we might say 'conserver') and is causing all matter to exist by His omnipotent power and sovereign will in every moment.

It would seem that this idea is not entirely new, even if, in my experience, it is rarely discussed. The philosopher Edward Feser explains that the Doctrine of Divine Conservation can be found in the writings of the Catholic theologian St. Thomas Aquinas. In the following quotation, he explains the Thomist perspective:

> The Doctrine of Divine Conservation (DDC) holds that the things that God has created could not continue in existence for an instant if He were not actively preserving them in being. DDC is a standard component of classical philosophical theology. St. Thomas Aquinas holds that:

> 'Now, from the fact that God rules things by His providence it follows that He preserves them in being... [T]o be is not the nature or essence of any created thing, but only of God... Therefore, no thing can remain in being if divine operation cease.' [Summa Contra Gentiles, Book III]...[2]

According to the Doctrine of Divine Conservation, then, God is not only creator, but also sustainer of all. The whole of existence, in this single eternal moment, is totally dependent on God, and nothing could remain in existence without Him.

The Doctrine of Occasionalism

Occasionalism is an idea associated with the French philosopher Nicolas Malebranche, who was influenced by the respective thought of St. Augustine and Descartes. The idea is similar to the Doctrine of Divine Conservation, but there are some differences. It's quite a complicated idea and I find the term a little clumsy but I will seek to explain my understanding of the concept as best as I can with the assistance of a few quotations.

According to the Internet Encyclopedia of Philosophy, "for the occasionalist, the regular operations of nature are governed by a system of occasional causes that cohere only on the basis of the regularity of God's will concerning them."[3]

Before I elaborate on what that means, let's also look at the International Society for the Study of Occasionalism's definition of Occasionalism:

[C]ontinuous creation may be interpreted in a way that denies the ascription of any causal power to finite beings. This is known as "occasionalism." According to this view, everything is created only by God at each moment, and no finite being has a causal role in creation. In other words, God is the sole causal agent.[4]

There is no doubt that we witness regularity in existence. If I strike a match, I expect to see fire. If I drop a ball, I expect it to hit the floor. But the idea here is that these things only happen on a particular occasion because God wills it to be so. In theory, I could strike my match and water could come out of it, or I could drop the ball and it might rise up to the ceiling. Regularity only exists because God is willing the same thing to happen on each occasion, hence the term *occasionalism*.

I am sure some of my Christian readers, believing the Bible to be the infallible Word of God, will be wondering where these ideas are evidenced in Scripture. Of course, these doctrines are not specifically named in the Bible, but it is certainly possible to argue from Scripture that all will is God's will.[5]

In conclusion, I am convinced that God is in sovereign control of the whole of creation, and that all of existence is a part of Him. The doctrines of Divine Conservation and Occasionalism serve to highlight the fact that wherever there is activity in existence, whether it be in the human body, in our actions, or in the movement of celestial bodies, God is the animating force behind that activity. He is not just creator, but sustainer. I believe that the doctrinal ideas explored here are helpful food for thought as we grapple with some of the most fundamental questions at the heart of the divine sovereignty versus human free will debate.

28

DIVINE OMNIPOTENCE AND FREE WILL

I have heard it argued that God's attribute of omnipotence must mean that He has the power and ability to bestow free will on His creatures, for if God were unable to create free creatures, is this not a limitation on His being that would diminish His omnipotence?

In response to this argument it's important for me to point out that I believe God is omnipotent only in respect of what is actually possible in reality. There *are* certain limitations, even on an omnipotent God. For instance, it would be impossible for God, who is omnipresent, to create another omnipresent God, because there would literally be no room for such a God. This could be seen as a limitation, though only if one were trying to apply a hypothetical situation to God.

Another example of a limitation on God is that He is unable to cease existing, because existence is part of His very nature.[1] This is quite a paradoxical limitation, because the very fact that God cannot cease to exist could be seen as a facet of His being related to His infinite power.

So, there are certain limitations that exist even in respect of an omnipotent God, although I would argue that within the cosmic playground in which we find ourselves, He is all-powerful.

In terms of how this relates to free will, my argument would be that God is unable to create free creatures, because there is nowhere in existence that is outside of the being of God (that's what literal omnipresence means), so there is literally no room for freedom from God, or free will. It is logically impossible for God to create free creatures, in the same way as it is logically impossible for God to create another omnipresent God, or to cease to exist, as I have argued above.

In relation to this argument I invite readers to

consider deeply what it would really mean to say you have free will. Did you freely choose the number of arms and legs you have, or the number of fingers you have on each hand? Are you circulating blood around your body, controlling your heartbeat, and growing your hair and nails? How is it that you are making thoughts arise in your mind, and emotions arise in your body?

When the above questions are explored in relation to one's present-moment experience, it should be obvious that we are not in control of ourselves at all. Instead, there is power in control of every aspect of our being. That power is God.

In Part 4, we have looked at the problem of free will from a range of different angles. Let us now turn our attention to the moral implications of my belief that everything that happens does so by the will of God.

PART V

MORALITY AND GOD

29

DIMENSIONS OF REALITY

Before we look in depth at the subject of morality, it will be helpful to give an overview of the way I believe reality is experienced by God and human beings respectively.

It is possible to view reality as though there are two separate dimensions. The first we will call *the God dimension*, and the second *the human dimension* (other creatures experience life in their own dimensions). The God dimension represents absolute awareness, which we can assume that God has all of the time. Everything in the universe, in the microcosm and the macrocosm, is present to God, and He perpetually coordinates the interaction of all the universe's various parts. The power and awareness necessary for this coordinating activity is immense, but it is right to assume that our creator has that power.

We might imagine that within the God dimension of reality, everything is clear and vibrant. In the human dimension, we get a snapshot of the total reality. Although we are an expression of the God dimension and are contained within it, our consciousness has limitations, such as those imposed by the body and its senses. The organism that is the body is a reality-limiting organism — it is as though we are only able to perceive things on a certain wavelength that is just a small part of the total spectrum of reality. Everything that we experience during human life occurs in the human dimension, but is also perceived by God in the ultimate dimension.

It is quite right to assume that things go on in the world all the time without us being aware of them. When I am writing these words, there must be countless processes going on both in my body and in the world at large that I am not aware of. It is God's infinite consciousness that is aware of the complete picture; we are only given a glimpse into what is going on at any one time.

Attributes of the human dimension include this limited awareness and also embodied emotions, sense perception, physical sensations, and thought. Attributes of the God dimension include the omnipotence, omnipresence, and omniscience described in the earlier chapter "What Are God's Attributes?".

It is possible that in the event of death, awareness expands from the human dimension to the God dimension. One could imagine this experience would be accompanied by a sense of relief, a kind of 'coming home' feeling, where once again the bigger picture is visible and everything makes sense.

Life in the human body never makes perfect sense. There is never a feeling that everything is perfectly okay, because we always have the problems of suffering and death to contend with. I would suggest that when our awareness expands from the human dimension to the God dimension in the event of death, the boundaries of human existence are seen to be illusory, and the beginning and ending of human life is seen in its right perspective, which is that, really, there is no birth and there is no death, only a continuation of a consciousness that has always existed and always will exist.

30

DO GOOD AND EVIL EXIST
OBJECTIVELY?

Even though all action is God's action, in the human dimension we still have the illusion of free will, and we therefore have choices and decisions to make. How do we decide what is good and evil, what is right and wrong?

Christians might argue that the Bible is the supreme revelation of God's moral direction for mankind. But the problem with this idea, from my perspective, is that God has created all books (including the Qur'an and other holy books). What, then, makes the ideas expressed in one holy book truer than those expressed in the others? It is possible to argue that many different scriptures which contradict one another are divinely revealed, so it is impossible to know which one we should regard as the absolute truth.

Thus, we cannot realistically argue that the Bible is the sole guide for moral action on this planet. Where else are we to look? From my perspective, this is problematic. It would seem that without moral guidance, we are living in a world where 'anything goes'. It is important to note, however, that it is not actually the case that anything goes. Only *God's will* goes. I have to admit that God includes rape, murder, torture, and other horrors as part of His action in the world. It may seem illogical for God to be involved with these things, but I believe that He has good reasons, as I will explain in the next two chapters.

So, it is not in fact the case that anything goes, but rather that everything is an expression of God's will. But it is also true that, along with the illusion of free will, we have the illusion of decision making and responsibility. We seem to live in societies, and we seem to be affected by the actions of others. There is nothing wrong, then, with creating laws that aim to protect people's wellbeing. In the absence of objective morality, this is a difficult, subjective process. It might involve prayer (that God guides us towards right action) and laws that aim to achieve the greatest happiness for everyone. There will, of course, be difficult moral decisions to make, and we must rely on God to guide us through these, always attempting to do what we feel is best in any given situation. Our decisions regarding what is best will have to be based on intuition, and compassion, which we must hope that God will grant us.

In summary, then, the realisation that God exists, and is in control of all things, creates a problem for moral discussion. The problem is that if we are not really in control, then how do we make decisions about right action? The answer in the dimension of ultimate reality is that God will take care of this. The answer in human terms is that we must struggle to do what we believe is right, all the while acknowledging that God is the guiding force in our decisions, and that nothing will ever happen outside of His sovereign will.

Some readers may feel that such a subjective approach to morality is unsatisfactory. But I would point out that even for those who adhere to the moral code of a sacred text, the words of the text must always be interpreted subjectively, so morality is never truly objective. I would also point out that my purpose in this book is not to try to discern which theology will theoretically produce the "best" or "most moral" society; I am concerned with simply espousing what I believe is the truth about God and His relationship with creation, and then exploring the moral implications which follow from that.

31

THE AGONY OF GOD

In this chapter, I would like to present my theory of two ways in which it is possible that God suffers, and I will go on to explain the relevance of this theory to our discussion of morality.

Firstly, God is supremely alone in the universe. All that exists is an expression of God's own self. In other words, God is really all that exists. Can you imagine what that must be like — never having another free being with whom to interact?

Secondly, God is unable to switch off. Existence is part of God's very nature. Therefore, for all eternity, God must live with the knowledge that there will never be an ending. Even if you have infinite power, as God does, how do you stay entertained and occupied for all eternity?

I believe that these two problems may amount to a kind of "hell" for God, and are perhaps the reason why God chooses to inflict suffering on human beings and all other forms of life on Earth. From this perspective, we might argue that God experiences both the yin and the yang of existence, the agony and the joy, the highs and the lows. God, therefore, makes us suffer in order to reflect His own predicament, so we get a taste of the real thing — of what ultimate reality is like for God.

There is a long history of attempting to come to terms with suffering in philosophy, from the Hedonism of Epicurus, to the Stoicism of Zeno, to the Utilitarianism of John Stuart Mill. Many philosophers have touched upon suffering in their writing, but all serious attempts to tackle the problem have fallen short of accounting for the seemingly gratuitous and unnecessary extent of suffering in the world. By understanding that God Himself suffers agony, we might have an insight that can help us to understand why God creates such terrible suffering in His creatures.

32

BRINGING GOOD OUT OF EVIL

In the preceding chapter, I argued that God might experience a certain kind of hell; the restrictions of being unable to 'switch off' from existence and the matter of being alone for all eternity might be a form of terrible suffering that God has to endure. I speculated that the reason why God makes His creatures suffer might be in order to give us a taste of His own suffering.

This is just a theory, however, and I believe it is perfectly possible that God doesn't suffer at all. Those who seek union with God through meditation and other spiritual disciplines often report experiencing a wonderful bliss in the deeper stages of their practice, and I myself have experienced something like this when I have been immersed in deep meditation. This leads me to wonder whether God's essence is perfect bliss, and whether He might be perfectly at peace in Himself, regardless of the 'limitations' on His being that I discussed above.

In the philosophy of Eastern religions such as Hinduism, it is often believed that we have an *I-it* relationship with God, as opposed to the *I-thou* relationship that is evident, for instance, in the Abrahamic religions. With an I-it relationship, God is *impersonal*, so it would make little sense to posit that God suffers from this perspective. With an I-thou relationship, God is *personal*, and so it's easier to imagine that God may experience suffering in a way that is similar to human persons. These two perspectives on the nature of God may appear to be in conflict, but there may be some truth contained in each. I believe this is one fascinating area for interfaith dialogue.[1]

I feel no shame in admitting that I don't understand everything about how God experiences reality. Although I believe God has given me certain insights into His nature, there are also aspects of His being that remain veiled to me, and that I believe I may only understand after the death of my body.

Whether or not God suffers is one such area where I feel at present I can only speculate.

That said, let us continue to explore why it may be that human beings often suffer so terribly.

If God doesn't make us suffer to give us a taste of His own suffering, then we must look for alternative explanations for why He makes us suffer. The argument that I find most compelling is that God always brings good out of evil.

It can be hard for us to understand why God might inflict rape, murder, torture, and other such horrors on His created subjects. I have myself experienced some intense episodes of suffering in my life, and have often questioned why God put me through them. But the evidence from my own life, and from countless other testimonies, is that our suffering is always under control, and limited. While God might make us suffer for a time, He always releases us from that suffering, whether it be through healing, through a turn of events, or in the form of death.

While the nature of the afterlife is, of course, mysterious to me, I have a hope that those who have suffered terribly in this life will encounter marvellous rewards in the next, and perhaps even a peace and joy that will totally eclipse the pain of any earthly suffering.

The drama of the intense highs and lows of creaturely life can be incredibly bewildering, but we must remember that we are unable to see the bigger picture that God sees. Most of us enjoy watching films or theatrical productions that depict a kind of emotional rollercoaster with a happy ending, and perhaps these stories are a microcosm of the story of an entire human life. Every life is different, of course, but if God didn't create a great diversity of experience (including both joy *and* suffering), perhaps reality, and the grand game that God is unfolding, would be less rich.

The whole of existence can be seen as a grand performance or play directed by God as a way of expressing and exploring the infinite possibilities that exist within His nature. The ability to inflict suffering seems to be an aspect of God's power that He likes to express, and I believe we should trust in His wisdom and that He has good reasons for making us suffer.

The evidence seems to me to suggest that although

people often suffer terribly, God is ultimately merciful and chooses to limit our suffering to what is necessary for His purposes and plans. My hope is that all who suffer will receive recompense for their hardship through the experience of an enduring joy and a peace that far outweighs their troubles.

33

DO WE ALL DESERVE HELL?

There is a common understanding among Christians that every human being is a sinner deserving of punishment in hell. The Christian worldview depicts human beings as wretched, sinful, lost, and in need of salvation. In this chapter, I want to examine this idea and whether it makes sense in light of the existence of a sovereign God.

I have often been puzzled by the Christian concept of original sin. The idea that a single rebellious action by one man, Adam, could lead to guilt for the whole human race for thousands of years seems somewhat bizarre. I can only imagine that the story of the fall of man must be metaphorical; a warning from God that each human being must guard against pride. Either that, or the fall is an idea created by theologians outside of Scripture, which has become popular simply because it is a way of justifying the Christian idea that every human being needs salvation.

As will have become clear over the earlier chapters of this book, I have a very high view of the sovereignty of God. I believe God is sovereign over all events. That is to say, we do not have free will. If you believe in free will, you are necessarily limiting the sovereignty of God. I am unwilling to do this because, when I contemplate the nature of God, I deduce that He is omnipresent and has no boundaries; there is no place where God ends and freedom begins. God is the creator, sustainer, and animator of all that exists.

It is not possible to be a Christian and believe what I have stated in the preceding paragraph. The whole Christian worldview hinges on the idea that we are guilty of punishment, and in order to be guilty, we must be free. Christians believe God is going to judge us for all of the decisions we have freely made. Without free will, the idea of divine judgment makes no sense, nor does the Christian worldview in general.

It all comes down to our understanding of the nature of God. What are His attributes? Is God separate from His creation, or is creation contained within God? Is God all-powerful or is His power limited? Is God everywhere, or is there a place where God's being ends and something else begins? Is God spirit, or matter, or spirit and matter?

What we understand and believe about God determines whether or not we can make sense of the Christian worldview and the idea that we are guilty sinners who deserve punishment in hell. I realise that for everyone who believes in God, this presents a predicament. I have explored this predicament in depth in my essay entitled "An Almighty Predicament".[1]

I have no reason to doubt that an all-powerful God could create hell: if He can make His creatures suffer agony in one moment (as I have experienced, and perhaps you have too), then it's possible He could make us suffer great distress for a very long span of time, even many thousands of years. However, if God is in control of everything we ever think and do throughout the entirety of our lives, then there is no room for the kind of moral culpability that might allow us to make sense of divine judgment. This gives me hope that the warnings about damnation issued by adherents to religions such as Christianity and Islam stem from a fundamental misunderstanding concerning the nature of God.

In this part of the book we have looked at the problems of suffering and evil, and I have offered some explanations concerning why these may be a comprehensible part of God's plan. In Part 6, we'll consider God's grand game from the point of view of science, and I'll share a few thoughts on the relationship between science and religion, and how they might both contain very useful insights that can contribute meaningfully to the future flourishing of human thought.

PART VI

SCIENCE AND GOD

34

WHY I BELIEVE IN GOD AND ALSO LOVE SCIENCE

My father, in his seventies at the time of writing, has spent the majority of his career working as a scientific editor, but he is also a practising Christian. He has no problem working on a book about Vitamin D deficiency during the week, and serving as a steward in his local church on the weekend.

I know my father wouldn't describe himself as a theologian, as theology has never been the focus of his studies or his work. For as long as I can remember, however, he has been actively involved with church life — singing in choirs, attending events, and sitting on committees.

I asked my father recently how he has been able to marry a long career as a scientific editor with his

Christian faith. I think he was rather surprised by the question, but after a little thought he paraphrased a saying commonly attributed to the British empiricist Francis Bacon: "A little thought inclines a man's mind to atheism, but depth in thinking brings one's mind around to religion."

I'm sure there are many atheist scientists who would be highly offended by such a statement, and, don't worry, I believe Bacon's statement is far from being a rule for everyone. Nevertheless, it's a saying that I could resonate with in terms of my own journey from atheism to faith, and perhaps there are others reading this book who can relate to it as well.

The moral of the story: if you're an atheist, your spiritual journey isn't necessarily over, so try to keep an open mind.

Despite his extensive experience as a scientific editor, my sense is that my father is able to accept the gospel of Jesus Christ in a simple and childlike way. This is not a criticism; Jesus himself said that in order to enter the Kingdom of Heaven we need to become like little children (Matthew 18:3). Perhaps, at the risk of putting words in my father's mouth, he feels as many people do that science is able to answer the *how* questions in life and religion is able to answer the *why* questions.

I didn't follow my father into the world of medical science, but I do heartily embrace the great achievements of science, and find the relationship between science and philosophy especially interesting. I am passionate about technology, and find advances in areas such as computer science and space exploration to be ceaselessly fascinating.

Since the time of the ancient Greek philosophers, questions concerning God and physical reality have been explored in tandem, and I see no reason why there can't be a fruitful relationship between the disciplines of science and religion in the future. I believe scientists can learn a lot from theologians, and theologians can learn a lot from scientists, so let's approach one another with humility and an eagerness to understand.

As part of my own contribution to such discussions, I will now present my reflections on a few ideas that are central to the scientific worldview, from my own philosophical perspective. I hope they will be of interest to philosophers and scientists alike.

35

CAUSE AND EFFECT

Causality is an idea so fundamental to science that, in a sense, it binds the scientific community together. Scientists have been able to formulate countless laws which have cause and effect as their basis.

I'm aware that my view of God, espoused in this book, presents a fundamental challenge to the idea of causality. I am not denying that scientists have accurately observed causes and effects happening in a way that instils great confidence in the scientific method, but what I will argue is that, in reality, causality is a myth.

It is important for the reader to closely examine what causality is. What we actually witness in the field of experience is not a succession of causes and effects, but a single unfolding. It would be impossible to say where one event ends and another begins, because all events flow into one another.

Let's take the example of me kicking a football. What caused the football to be kicked? Was it my foot striking the ball, my run up to the ball, my arrival at the football pitch, my birth into existence, or the 'Big Bang'? It is impossible to say. The confusion comes from the very differentiation of the eternal process into separate events.

I am not denying that we observe a high degree of regularity in many aspects of the observable universe, but what I will argue is that God is above the laws of physics and could, if He so willed, change the way causes are effected in any instance.

One thing that gives me great confidence in this theory is my observation of my own dreams. Dreams can seem just as real as waking life, yet the rules of nature can be completely different within a dream. Also, as recounted in earlier chapters of this book, I have witnessed miraculous happenings that defy the laws of nature. This is sufficient evidence for me to understand that God is controlling all so-called cause-and-effect occurrences, and could change the outcome of an event on any occasion, if that were His will.

In summary, then, the fact that event 'B' follows event 'A' doesn't prove that event 'A' caused event 'B', and this is a really important thing for philosophers and scientists to realise. Every day we observe night following day and day following night, but this doesn't mean that day is the cause of night or that night is the cause of day. Events are bound up with our concept of time, and when we realise that time is illusory, it is easy to see that events are too. I will have more to say on this in the next chapter.

I believe that everything that is certain in science is actually incredibly fragile, for in any moment, God has the ability to stir things up and demonstrate His power over the laws of nature. Theists believe God does this regularly throughout history via the working of miracles, and scientists would do well to take note. In a world of infinite possibilities, I would suggest it's unwise to posit that effect 'B' *always* follows cause 'A'.

36

REFLECTIONS ON TIME

In the modern world we are obsessed with the idea that the past leads to the future. This is a complete myth, perhaps the biggest of our age. It is a presumption on which so much science is based, and it pervades our culture as well.

Have you ever wondered why there are 60 minutes in an hour but 24 hours in a day? Seconds, minutes, hours, days, months, years — all of these are artificial creations which have no reality. A simple experiment will help demonstrate this, if you feel like giving it a go. Start by discarding all the clocks, watches, or other time-measuring instruments you have in the room. Then, quite simply, try to time a minute. Clap your hands to start, and clap again to stop.

So, experiment over, how successful were you? The first thing to realise is that you will never know. It is significant that you will never know because what that tells us is that time is not inside you. You have no way of knowing what a second or a minute or an hour or a month is, independent of some measuring device.

The conclusion we can draw from this is that time is encapsulated in measuring devices, rather than in reality. This might sound obvious to some people, but will be a shocking assertion to others. For if there is no time, how can we talk meaningfully about things as having beginnings?

I would ask you to consider this. What is the beginning of the elephant? Is it the baby elephant? Is it the fetal elephant? Is it the sperm of the elephant's father, and the egg of its mother, perhaps? Or is it the elephant's father and mother? Or the grandparents of the elephant? We can go back in 'time' forever trying to establish what first caused the elephant, but we won't get anywhere because what we are doing is fabricating. We are creating ideas about a past that doesn't exist. It is a futile task. There is an adult elephant that is manifesting now and that is all that we can meaningfully say without conjecture.

I realise that this way of looking at the world has far-reaching implications. It has implications for science, in terms of how useful attempts are to discover how the universe began, for instance. It has implications for talking therapies like psychotherapy and psychoanalysis, which attempt to look at the present in terms of the past, and see one's present as the result of childhood experiences, for instance.

But maybe we need to shift our focus in the Western World. Maybe we have become so enamoured by time that we have become dependent on it, forgetting all the while its limitations as being a mechanism rather than a reality.

It is liberating to remember that we exist outside of time, as bondage to the past and to the future creates a kind of structure in our lives that can inhibit our experience of the present moment, which contains the fullness of God and is all there really is.

37

WHAT IS TRUTH?

In an earlier chapter, I described some of the things that our dreams can tell us about reality, and I would now like to expand on this further in relation to the subject of truth.

Perhaps you will be able to recall from your own experience that, not only is it possible for the laws of physics to be different in dreams, it is also possible for our background and our life experiences to be different in dreams. For example, in a dream, we may recall that we went to a certain school or university that, in waking reality, we recognise to be entirely fictional. We may be married to someone in a dream, and have a sense that we know that person intimately and deeply, yet when we wake up, we are able to see that our dream-time spouse is actually someone who we have never met, and who may not even exist in waking reality.

I have argued that dreams can feel just as 'real' as waking life, and that we have no reason for believing that the experiences we have in dreams are any less real than the situations we encounter in waking life. The above examples of possible dream scenarios show that everything that we feel constitutes our 'selves', including such seemingly stable things as our life experiences and our relationships, are actually no more than mere impressions in consciousness, held in our minds for a time by God, but which could be altered or eradicated by God at any time.

God can make such impressions endure over time if He wishes, as is the case with what He does in our waking lives, where we may feel we are the 'same person' for 80 years, for instance. Time is an illusion though, and that is also relevant here. We may imagine our 'past' to be something very tangible, but the truth is that everything we feel constitutes our human life is just an impression in consciousness in the present moment, held in one's mind by God, and He could take it away in an instant if He so desired.

While I might feel myself to be Steven Colborne, and might associate that name with a whole story, everything that constitutes that story has no basis or grounding in reality; it is merely a thought.

The above considerations are deeply relevant to the question 'What is truth?', as in any given situation, God may bring to our minds a certain 'memory' of a situation that is entirely new, and we would have no way of knowing this was happening.

Some people who experience psychosis have what are known as 'false memories'. For instance, during an episode of psychosis, someone might have a memory of a crime they committed, and fear being arrested for it, when in reality the events they are 'remembering' never happened. In such situations, someone may wholeheartedly believe they are recalling the truth, yet, in reality, God is bringing a fabricated scenario to their minds and could change their recollections of past 'events' at any time. There is no reason why such fabrications should be limited to people with a diagnosis of psychosis; God is in control of all our minds and lives and not just those people to whom a doctor has given a certain diagnostic label.

The fact that false memories can happen has important real-world implications. It is relevant in relation to the justice system, for instance, because in a courtroom scenario there is often a focus on trying to ascertain whether or not something actually happened. Anyone (including those on trial, judges, or members of a jury) might have an idea in their mind that feels like a truthful understanding or recollection of a situation but is actually a complete fabrication. This is in keeping with the vision of God I have described throughout this book, where I have depicted God as being entirely in control of our thoughts and everything that exists in reality.

Considerations in this chapter may lead the reader to the conclusion that I am advocating for a kind of 'post-truth anarchy', where nothing really exists and everything is subjective. But the question should not be what I am *advocating*; I am merely attempting to describe the truth of reality, as God has given me understanding. If my vision resonates with you in some way, perhaps that is because you recognize that there is truth in what I am saying. That will all depend upon the impressions God is making in your mind as you read these words, and as you reflect, which I can neither predict nor be held accountable for.

I admit there is a kind of 'chaos' to my philosophy,[1] but this is just an honest reflection of the way the world really is. The world can also be seen to be very ordered, from a certain perspective, and God does seem to make certain modes of mind and certain physical objects endure over long periods of time, which is why the laws of physics often seem to be so consistent. So, post-truth anarchy is only one way of looking at things.

What I'd like for readers to take away from this chapter is an understanding that, upon close examination, firm convictions we may hold concerning what constitutes 'truth' are actually more fluid and flexible than many people suppose. It is God who is determining what we believe to be truth at any given time. There are implications for this understanding in the real world, and I invite readers to carefully consider their own beliefs concerning what constitutes 'truth' in relation to the ideas expressed here.

38

CREATION AND EVOLUTION

I am aware that true scientists recognise they are only ever working with theories. Theories in science are always open to revision when empirical evidence does not support them, and this is in line with the principle of falsifiability espoused by the philosopher Karl Popper.[1]

A theory that is currently very popular in the scientific world is that the universe came into existence from an infinitesimally small point that, for an unknown reason, exploded into existence in an event known as the 'Big Bang'. While this theory might be in-keeping with certain scientific observations, I believe it to be highly problematic when considered philosophically. For instance, if one posits that the universe began at a single point, what was surrounding that point? To speak of a point is to use spatial language, and a point only makes sense in the context of what surrounds it. There is also the significant problem of what existed before such a singularity.

I really struggle to imagine that a universe full of complexity and diversity — a universe in which we are able to go to the theatre, listen to a symphony, or fall in love — can be attributed to an infinitely dense point spewed out of the universe 14 billion years ago. It seems absurd.

Then again, the story of creation we find in Genesis, with all its apparent inconsistencies and mythical qualities, seems unlikely as well.

My own theory of creation is somewhat less magical than either the 'Big Bang' theory or the Genesis account. Believing as I do that God has existed eternally means He has had a *lot* of time for trial and error when it comes to creation. It's interesting that Christians say God created man in His own image, because if this is true, maybe we can learn something about creation from human behaviour?

When I'm engaged in a creative project, I normally have a range of ideas swirling around my mind, and I will brainstorm things and make notes and start to form a plan. I will try things out, and often fail and have to start again from scratch. Could I be so bold as to suggest that the creative process might be similar for God?

Allow me to quote for you a passage from my book *The Philosophy of a Mad Man* in order to illustrate this theory:

> Imagine if you were God, and had all power, all knowledge, and all things at your disposal. You could do absolutely anything, with the only limitation being that nothing could ever be separate from you. What would you do?
>
> You might start off with a pure 100% awareness of your simplest form, God. This would be a you without any of the attributes we associate with objects, and only you. No time, no space. Pure aliveness, pure nothingness, pure God.
>
> You might want to experiment with this aliveness, and begin by creating a few things, simple things. You might cause part of yourself to be bright and

call it light, and another part dim and call it darkness. That might satisfy you for some time, but then you may feel a desire to experiment further, and realise that by altering part of yourself you can create different shades of light, or colours. You might create a rainbow of light the size of a universe. How enjoyable and fascinating this would be to do!

And then, after playing around with light and colour for a few millennia, you might want a new challenge. And so you start condensing parts of yourself into a solid form called matter, and create a few different shapes, simple shapes. And then you realise that by holding a distilled part of yourself in a certain way, you can give the appearance of objects. You can create as many as you want, move them around, and even thrust them into each other! You might well marvel at your creation.

And then, as the aeons pass by, you have the most incredible, wonderful idea. You could create complex objects and create within them the impression that they are entities-in-themselves; that like you, they are beings! They could even interact with each other. You could be the grand puppeteer in a huge universe filled with creatures, and you could create the creatures in such a way that they don't even have to know you exist. So overjoyed would you be with this idea that you would create thousands and then millions of these things in different forms, and give them all names.

You decide to give the people that you create the experience of emotions, in order to reflect the spectrum of reality that exists within your own experience. Like you, your creations will experience wholeness and bliss, but also loneliness and isolation. You hold within your nature both the bliss of absolute consciousness, and the pain of being eternally alone, and you decide that your creations will experience both aspects of your predicament in order to get a taste of the yin and yang of existence.

But still, your potential for elaboration on these marvellous creations is unfulfilled, and you wonder what you should do next. How about a story, you say. Everyone knows that a story needs a beginning, a middle, and an end, and so you invent time and memory, to give the impression that things are moving along. How marvellous all this is, you think to yourself.

And so you come up with a storyline that will last for thousands of years, and that comprises a wonderful display of who you are through your creation. You decide that you will use a single being that you have created in order to display your infinite power and ultimately loving nature. So you create a man named Jesus Christ, who embodies so much of what you are, and you call him your Son. You make him famous on Earth, and display your love for him and for other human beings through miracles, through healing, and through compassion. Through your human creations you make a book about this man and his life, where the story can be captured. The book, called The Bible, is perfect in its imperfection, as is the case with all that you so delicately and masterfully create (Oh how you love to give the impression of independence, frailty, and free will!)

You use the story of Jesus Christ as a means of reconciliation, of bringing people who you have caused to feel separate from you back into a knowledge of and relationship with you. You call this salvation, and make it the purpose of human life on Earth.[2]

I realise this theory is imperfect in many ways. For instance, it assumes that there was a starting point, which, with an eternal God, is impossible. There can, of course, be a starting point to what we describe as this particular universe, but not to God's creativity in general. Admittedly, eternity is a difficult concept for any human being to fathom (the idea that God might have been creating universes for an infinitely long time).

Also, I don't know whether Jesus Christ is really the centrepiece in God's grand plan, as Christians would argue and as I believed when I wrote the above-quoted piece. A 2000-year reign may seem like an incredibly long time that would justify the argument, but in the context of eternity, this span of time is a mere moment.

I believe we should all exercise some humility when it comes to theories concerning how the universe began. It's highly likely, in my view, that the 'Big Bang' theory will be eclipsed by more sophisticated theories, and it could be that the solution to this conundrum is something God only reveals in the life to come.

In Part 6 I have offered a few reflections on how some of the leading ideas in the world of science relate to my own worldview. Not being a scientist myself, I have kept these reflections fairly general, only highlighting those areas where I believe my philosophical perspective is particularly relevant.

I believe there is plenty of opportunity for future dialogue between scientists and theologians in relation to the subject matter discussed in this book. One particularly interesting area for further research that comes to mind would be that of indeterminacy in quantum mechanics. Understanding that God is the present-moment animator of all events will inevitably cast light on the idea of indeterminacy and some of the other fundamental problems of quantum physics that scientists are grappling with in our time.

In Part 7, let us turn our attention to the broad question of how my philosophy relates to the major religious traditions that have not yet been considered in this book.

PART VII

MY PHILOSOPHY AND THE
WORLD RELIGIONS

39

INTRODUCTION

In this book so far, we have explored the nature of God, and the grand game He is unfolding, from a variety of different angles. When talking about religion, I have focused mostly on Christian theology. There are several reasons for this. Firstly, Christianity is currently the biggest religion on the planet. Secondly, Christianity has played a large role in my own spiritual journey. Thirdly, I am a Westerner, and Christianity is the predominant religion in the West.

In Part 7, I would like to discuss some important beliefs found in other major world religions, and how those beliefs relate to my own views concerning the God/world relationship.

I have not had the same involvement with the other

world religions discussed here as I have had with Christianity, and I do not profess to be an expert in religions such as Hinduism, Judaism, and Islam, although I have studied these religions to some extent and am familiar with their key doctrines and beliefs. Interfaith dialogue is an area of great interest to me, and I hope that I will be able to learn much more about these other religions as my spiritual journey progresses. That said, in this part of the book I will share some insights into the world religions as I understand them, and will describe how some of the key beliefs found in these religions relate to my vision of God as cosmic animator.

40

THE ABRAHAMIC RELIGIONS

It is not just Christians who believe we are free to act independently of the will of God. We find this idea in all of the major Abrahamic religions (Christianity, Islam, and Judaism). It is clear that the Old Testament, which adherents to all three of these religions believe is Holy Scripture, encapsulates the notion of human free will. God issues commandments and then human beings are free to respond to those commandments. Depending on how humans respond, they are then judged by God, who will reward or punish them for their actions. It is important to note that both Christians and Muslims maintain that non-belief will result in punishment in hell.

As I have argued throughout this work, it is not

logical that a God who is omnipresent can create free creatures. In reality, the entirety of creation exists and is sustained by the will of God. When people do not believe in a particular religion, it is God who is creating their disbelief. The idea of punishment is therefore ridiculous, as God would be punishing human beings for His own action.

In conclusion, then, my argument that we do not have free will is of crucial philosophical importance because it sheds light on the illogical nature of ideas like divine commandment and judgment that are central to the Old Testament and to the Abrahamic religions.

41

THERE IS NO ENLIGHTENMENT

The word 'enlightenment' is central to the beliefs of millions of Buddhists, Hindus, and other religious adherents with an interest in Eastern philosophy. The term is somewhat mysterious, but refers to a mystical state that certain spiritual masters are said to have attained which has freed them from bondage to the suffering associated with worldly things. In this chapter I would like to talk about my personal experience with the idea of enlightenment, which has played a significant role in my spiritual journey.

When I was studying for my undergraduate degree, I used to spend a lot of time meditating. I would focus on my breathing, and attempt to simply observe, without any effort, what was going on in my body and in my mind. This was a regular practice for a few years, and I sometimes experienced feelings of peace and calmness. On one occasion, I had a deep spiritual experience, and I witnessed my bodily form dissolving into a feeling of bliss. The feeling only lasted a few seconds, before I came back down to earth and began reflecting on what I had experienced. I don't know whether meditation gets much deeper than that.

I was definitely trying to 'get somewhere' with my meditation practice. I was desperate for peace. In a sense, I was trying to escape. It wasn't until, after years of struggling, when I finally decided to give psychotherapy a try, that I began to realise what I was trying to escape from.

No doubt, I was a mess when I began attending psychotherapy. My mother had passed away after a terrible illness, and I was still merged with my mother in the way that children tend to be merged with their parents. I had loved my mother dearly and had been obsessive about looking after her, but in the meantime, I had lost a great deal of myself. What psychotherapy did was begin to put me back in touch with myself.

As I explored my frustrations, fears, anger, and suffering, I began to find words to convey to my psychotherapist the deep loneliness that I had felt for many years. With frequent tearful outbursts, I began to talk through emotions that had been repressed, and I began to be much more self-aware. A big part of being an adult is simply finding words to express emotions. This is something I never learned how to do as a child, and it was liberating to learn how to do so as an adult.

The more I attended psychotherapy, the less interested I was in meditation and enlightenment. This is because I was finding the peace that I had been seeking through meditation in my new abilities to express myself openly and be in touch with my feelings. It surprised me that the enlightenment I had been striving so hard to attain became relatively unimportant. All I had really needed was to explore what my fear of not being enlightened meant in terms of my past and my present emotions.

When God began to reveal Himself to me in my mid-twenties, this brought a whole new dimension to my life. The reality of God puts the idea of meditation in a completely different perspective. I became aware that the supreme reality was not just a feeling of bliss; it was an active God. I realised that God is in control of everything, from the movement of thoughts to the movement of celestial bodies.

What troubles me about meditation is that it tends to neglect God as doer, as it focuses so intently on what can be personally achieved. I also believe it can be an attempt to escape from emotional states that we are afraid of.

It bothers me that there are people who consider themselves to be spiritual gurus who have supposedly attained enlightenment, because I can now see clearly that there is no such thing. Having doubts, frustrations, and fears is simply part of life — there is no magical state where we are free from these things. We wouldn't be human if we didn't experience these emotions.

There is no supreme peace in this life; we are all in touch with other people, who have their own problems, and we have to deal with them. Even if you sit under a tree for decades and meditate, you are still 100% dependent on God for any peace of mind that you experience. God can bring or take away your peace in any moment, so no one has ever really attained stable peace or enlightenment.

If anyone claims to you that they are enlightened, alarm bells should ring in your mind, and you should ask that person to explain precisely what they mean. If it doesn't make sense to you, on your terms, then you must reject the idea. It is quite probable that the supposedly enlightened person is deluded.

There is a culture in India where those who are supposedly more enlightened gain devotees and win the respect of many people. This is analogous to the pop stars of the West, in that people's devotion can become obsessive. But please realise that the so-called 'enlightened one' has absolutely nothing to offer you. Don't think that they are great. Don't think that they are special. In the same way that the guru is a child of God, so are you. The guru has nothing that you don't have.

There is no enlightenment. The reality is that your happiness or sadness in this eternal moment is totally dependent upon the will of your creator and sustainer, Almighty God.

42

KARMA

Many Indian religious traditions, including Hinduism, Sikhism, and Buddhism, have the idea of karma as one of their core beliefs.

Although there are nuances and variations in the way karma is perceived between these different religions, the key ideas about karma are common to all of them.

Karma is the idea that there are consequences to all of our actions. A good deed or act reaps future happiness, and similarly, a bad deed will reap future suffering. The things that we do affect the things that we experience in the future.

The first obvious problem with this idea is that good

and bad are subjective terms. Whenever we speak of good and bad, we must always ask: good and bad according to whom? There is no absolute good or badness in the world. Therefore, a believer in karma could never know whether they were doing good or bad, which is a significant problem.

The next problem with the idea of karma concerns free will. In a sense, the Indian religions have created the same problem as we find in the Abrahamic religions. In both schools of thought, we have the idea that some actions are freely undertaken and others are the result of an outside moral force which has the power of judgement and of inflicting repercussions.

The dividing line between what is free action and what is not free is disastrously unclear. For instance, if, at a certain moment in time, one is experiencing the consequences of previous actions, one would have to argue that there is no freedom in that moment. But what has happened to the freedom that existed previously? It doesn't make sense.

Both the Abrahamic religions and the Indian religions say there are moral consequences to freely undertaken actions. The only question is whether those consequences are the result of God's will (as in the Abrahamic religions) or of some kind of natural cause-and-effect law (as some Indians who do not believe in God would argue).

It is hard to see how some kind of natural karmic law could understand good and bad, which are subjective moral ideas that depend on the perspective of a personal agent, be that agent a human being or God. Therefore, the idea of a natural karmic law is problematic. For all those who do believe in God, it is vital to deeply consider God's attributes. If God is omnipotent and omnipresent, as many theologians propose, and as I have argued throughout this book, then there cannot be free will, which is the foundation of the idea of karma.

A further problem with the idea of karma is that it is a myth that one event leads to another.[1] Because God is omnipresent and therefore actively in control of everything that happens, event 'A' will only lead to consequence 'B' if God decides for that to happen on any particular occasion. There are no absolute laws of cause and effect outside of the will of God. In any case, cause and effect are just ideas in the mind of a perceiver. In reality, because events flow into one another and have no boundaries, there are no separate events. There is one eternal moment that does not contain intrinsic divisions into 'past' and 'future', which are mere concepts. Therefore, the whole idea of karmic consequence is deeply problematic.

If one considers the arguments in this chapter and elsewhere in this book, it is easy to see that the idea of karma is illogical. This means that one of the central convictions of the major Indian religions is mistaken.

I do not mean to idly dismiss the beliefs of millions of people. I have a deep respect for religious people of all persuasions, believing as I do that their beliefs come from God and are a part of His grand game. My purpose in this chapter is merely to point out that often cherished beliefs, such as the idea of karma, can be seen to be irrational when the true nature of God is deeply considered, and that is something I have tried to do without bias throughout this book.

43

POLYTHEISM

Polytheism is the belief in multiple deities, and has played an important role in the history of religion. The ancient Greeks believed in a pantheon of gods and goddesses, and in the East the ancient religion of Hinduism developed a complex system of deities, at least in some of its myriad expressions.

It is important to point out that those who believe in multiple gods often believe there are lesser gods who are expressions or aspects of the one true God. For example, in some forms of Hinduism, the concept of Brahman (found in the sacred Vedas) is the principle of ultimate reality that finds expression in lesser deities such as Shiva and Vishnu, each of whom serve to embody different aspects of the divine nature.

It seems that the ancient Romans, by way of contrast, had a more literal view of gods as actual physically embodied beings with very human characteristics, as is evident from the way they portrayed their gods in surviving works of ancient Roman art and literature.

The recurring theme at the heart of this book — that there is one God in control of all activity in existence — is certainly in tension with the idea that multiple deities could exist in any literal way. In order to embrace polytheism, we would have to deny many of the attributes which are definitional of God, and which were described in the chapter entitled "What are God's Attributes?", including His omnipotence and omnipresence.

The only way I can conceive of polytheism making sense is if every lesser god that exists is under the direct control of the one true God, in the same way that all human beings, according to my arguments throughout this book, are under God's direct control. The lesser gods would have to be like puppets in the metaphorical hands of the one true God, as I believe all creatures are.

One idea that I touched upon briefly in Part 3 is that the nature of God, and therefore existence, must essentially be *simple*. I feel unable to reconcile what appears to be order and harmony in creation (as displayed, for instance, in the consistent operation of the laws of physics), with the idea that multiple extremely powerful gods coexist. There would only ever be chaos in such a worldview, and surely one of the multiple deities would come to dominate and eradicate the others. And, of course, there is the further significant problem of how such deities would have come into existence in the first place. I feel that speculations about cosmic warfare between deities need not even be entertained, because, as already explained, the supposed existence of multiple divine beings with free will entails an illogical denial of God's fundamental attributes.

There may well be realms, or dimensions, in which beings that we don't associate with our regular experience of the waking world exist. Spiritual beings, such as angels and demons, might exist in these other dimensions. I have heard, for example, personal testimonies of people acquiring the special ability to see such spiritual beings even within our own world, and I have no reason to believe such experiences are not genuine. God's omnipotence means He is surely equipped to create an amazing diversity of beings, some of which may not be perceptible in the normal everyday experiences of waking human life.

But the important point to make is that other spiritual beings, including other deities, could not exist separately from, or in conflict with, the one true God. This should be an understanding that provides comfort to anyone who might be concerned that they are caught up in some kind of spiritual battle between different deities, or the forces of good and evil, as is so often the way reality is portrayed in culture and in various religious traditions. Such people can rest assured that logically there can only be one God, and nothing can happen that is outside of His sovereign will, despite any manifestations that He might use within the cosmic playground to bring interest and diversity to His creation as part of the unfolding of His grand game.

44

INTERFAITH DIALOGUE

There are many rich areas of common interest between the major Abrahamic and the great Eastern religions. In this chapter, I will briefly offer a few examples, in an attempt to persuade readers that interreligious dialogue has the potential to be deeply interesting and fruitful.

One key principle that can be found in nearly all the major world religions is what is known as the Golden Rule. This was expressed famously in its positive form by Jesus during the Sermon on the Mount, when He said, "Thou shalt love thy neighbour as thyself" (Matthew 22:39). The commandment is also found at the centre of the central book of the Jewish Torah (Leviticus 19:18). In Confucianism, the Ancient Chinese religion, the same principle is expressed in its negative form: "What you do not desire for yourself, do not do to others."[1] This cornerstone of moral conduct, therefore, represents common ground among diverse religious groups from across the world.

Belief in an afterlife represents another area of common ground between many of the world religions, though their perceptions of what the afterlife entails differ greatly. For instance, Hindus believe in the transmigration of souls; we can be reborn as other forms of life, or experience another human rebirth. Many people in Africa believe in reincarnation, where it is believed to preserve the continuity of the family line, so people are reborn into the same family. Christians, taking a different view, believe in a heavenly realm, where the believer who has died will live on in a resurrected body which will exist eternally.

Although these ideas around life after death are very different, they are similar in that, unlike the common atheist position, which sees the human person as purely material and therefore unable to persist after death, they agree that death doesn't mark the end of the human being, but that there is a continuation of consciousness in some form. This is an area where there may be rich and fruitful dialogue between people of different religious persuasions.

Another area that represents a possibility for interreligious dialogue is the oneness of God. An important element of Jewish worship services is the recitation of the *Shema*, a proclamation which is found in the book of Deuteronomy (6:4): "Hear, O Israel: the Lord our God, the Lord is One." In Islam, the idea of the unity of God is called *tawhid*. Many Sufis (Sufism is the more mystical branch of Islam) believe in the idea of *wahdat al-wujud*, literally translated as "unity of being". This doctrine teaches that the entire universe is God. This view is similar to pantheism, an idea prominent in the Eastern religions, and to my own view of God as described throughout this book. Here, then, we have another fascinating topic for interreligious dialogue.

And another example. There is debate in Islam over whether the Qur'an is created or eternal. Similarly, in Christianity there is debate over whether the three persons of the Trinity are eternal. I would argue, then, that there is room for fruitful debate between Christians and Muslims concerning what is created and what is eternal.

When considering the relationship between Christianity and Islam, it's important to consider Abraham, who plays a central role in the Scriptures of both religions. According to the Bible, Abraham was given a promise that from his son Ishmael would come a great nation (Genesis 17:20). The descendants of Ishmael, as well as the other sons of Abraham through Keturah, are referred to as the children or people of the east. They are the progenitors of the Arabs, from which the lineage of Muhammad, the esteemed prophet of Islam, can be traced. Taking this into consideration, one might surmise that even within the Christian Scriptures, God made it clear that he had a very important role for Islam in the grand plan of creation. Of course, this is a claim that will provoke a great deal of speculation, but such speculation is important and is fertile ground for dialogue between these two great religions.

Throughout the history of civilization there has always existed a diversity of religious perspectives across the world, and this has resulted in terrible conflict and a huge amount of bloodshed as people have fought to defend the veracity of their beliefs against those of their opponents.

I believe we are now in an age where the world has become a lot smaller (metaphorically speaking) due to advanced methods of travel and technological innovations such as the internet. This means that there is more opportunity for engagement between people of different faith backgrounds than ever before.

Throughout history, religions have often looked backwards rather than forwards, but I believe that this is something that needs to change if mankind is to prosper in the future. The challenges of the twenty-first century include the very survival of our planet, which faces threats including global warming and the proliferation of nuclear weapons that have the potential to cause mass death and destruction on an unthinkable scale.

I believe that now is the time for the religions of the world to set aside their differences and focus on what they have in common. If we can only recognise that we are members of a single human race, which has a future beyond the confines of our native planet, then we can embrace the wonderful diversity of all that God has done through religion in human history and find a way for faith in the one true God to flourish like never before.

With the above principles in mind, I would like to close with what I believe is the most important chapter of the book, in which I present a vision of what the religious future of human beings might entail.

PART VIII

THE CHURCH OF THE FUTURE

45

THE CHURCH OF THE FUTURE

If you relate to my philosophy and share my views regarding the nature of God, you may well question where your religious affiliations should lie. There is no existing religion that I am aware of in which the omnipresent nature of God, and the fact that there is no free will, are fully embraced. There is no major institution that looks to the future and provides an environment for discussing the relationship between science, the world religions, and the future of the human race.

With the above considerations in mind, I believe that we need a new church for humanity. Remember that the word 'church' simply means 'community', and although people with a Christian background would be welcome in the church that I envisage, it would not be a Christian church. It would be a church that exists for everyone who believes in the one true God.

The name that I propose for this new church is *The Universal Church of Almighty God*.

I have dedicated some time to thinking about what a truly magnificent church of the future might be like, and here are a few ideas.

Backward- and Forward-looking

The church will celebrate the past, embracing the rich and diverse history of humanity, but it will also look to the future, planning ahead and imagining what potential the human race can achieve.

In terms of the past, the church will embrace the history of philosophy and religion, celebrating the most important Scriptures of different religions and the most important works in philosophy, literature, and science. Human achievement, across all disciplines, will be celebrated.

In terms of the future, the church will seek to contribute to the advancement of science and technology in line with humanity's highest aspirations. The church will be a place for the discussion of ethical and moral questions related to human progress. Part of the role of the church will be to explore and imagine where the human race is heading, and to prepare people psychologically and spiritually for the future.

A Universal Perspective

There is no doubt that science and technology are advancing at an astonishing rate, and we should be proud of the things that scientists have achieved and are achieving. With new discoveries in quantum physics happening all the time, I believe it is only a matter of time before further discoveries allow us to create new technologies that will revolutionise space travel, allowing us to journey much deeper into space than ever before.

With such a vast universe existing, and knowing the infinite creative potential of God, I believe that there are probably beings on other planets. It is highly likely that the future of God's plan for humanity will not confine us to Earth, but will involve us settling on other planets, and interacting with other creatures. Earth will be viewed by history as humanity's first planet, in the days when we thought we were alone in the universe.

Part of the role of the new church that I envisage will be to celebrate discoveries in science and technology, and reflect on the philosophical importance of those discoveries. We may discuss, for instance, the way society might develop on humanity's second planet, and the way we should behave when we encounter other beings and other races in the universe.

Art and Culture

I believe that the new church should be a place to celebrate art and culture. There should be a stage in each church building for theatre, music, dance, opera, and other performances. The stage can employ advanced lighting and sound systems so that truly spectacular performances can be achieved. Part of the role of the church will be to celebrate everything that makes us human, and art is a wonderful way of doing this.

Beautiful Buildings

I believe that the church of the future should be at the cutting edge of construction technology. We can make beautiful buildings that draw upon the finest architecture in the world and praise God through their sheer magnificence. I envisage golden domes and vibrant and beautiful colours in glorious stained-glass windows that depict key moments in human religious and scientific history, with laser lighting that creates a wonderful atmosphere both inside and outside the church building.

Everyone is welcome

As I have already mentioned, the church will exist for everyone who believes in the one true God. People of all cultures, nationalities and religious backgrounds will be invited to come together to celebrate humanity and engage in worship. In truth, there is one God who has created the people of all religions, and the new church will be a place to set aside religious differences and embrace the one thing that every being in the universe has in common: we are created, sustained and animated by the same God.

Equality

Historically, religion has been associated with sexual inequality. In Christianity, for instance, there are centuries-old disputes about whether women should be priests or bishops. In Islam, men and women tend to be separated during prayer.

In the church of the future there will be equal opportunities for men and women. They will be able to pray and worship God together, and their roles within the church will be discerned on the grounds of passion and expertise rather than which sex they happen to be. People of all sexual orientations will be welcomed into the church and it will be acknowledged that God has created everyone to be the way they are.

Peace and Unity

A key focus of the new church will be to avoid further conflict around the world and to promote peace and unity among nations. By celebrating the things that are common to all human beings, we can embrace a vision for all of humanity, rather than pursuing separate visions for different religions and different nations. Technology such as the internet is already leading to a greater sense of global community, and The Universal Church of Almighty God can be the institution that turns the *virtual* global community into a *real* global community.

Let us be bold in our thinking and imagine how wonderful the church of the future could be. We all have a role to play in the unfolding of humanity's future, and whether or not this church becomes a reality is up to you.

ACKNOWLEDGEMENTS

Firstly, and most importantly, I would like to thank God for the inspiration that has brought this book into being. All glory to Almighty God forever. I would also like to thank Sarah for being an exceptional editor, Jet for being an inspiring and inspired cover designer, and the folks at ALLi for their advice and support.

I'd like to thank my beta readers David and Graham for providing invaluable feedback, and Hannah for her help with the strategy side of things. Thanks also to everyone who has provided emotional support and encouragement throughout the project, including Lu, Catherine, Dominic, Kieran, and many others.

Finally, many thanks to my family: my sister Femke for being so generous to me during tough times, my father Andrew towards whom I hold no hard feelings, and my grandparents Riet and Jarig whose financial support made this project possible.

THANK YOU FOR READING

If you enjoyed this book, please consider leaving a positive review on Amazon. It needn't be a long review — even a few words would be appreciated!

WEB LINKS AND CONTACT DETAILS

Steven runs a philosophy and theology blog, where a vibrant community of deep thinkers discuss life's big questions. Visit the blog at www.perfectchaos.org

Steven has a YouTube channel with videos reflecting on a range of philosophical and theological subjects related to the content of this book. You can visit and subscribe to the channel at www.youtube.com/c/stevencolborne

If you're inspired by Steven's vision for a new church – The Universal Church of Almighty God – you are invited to find out more and to consider participating. Visit the church website at www.tucoag.org

You're welcome to visit Steven's personal website, from where you can connect with him on social media or email him directly. The site can be found at www.stevencolborne.com

ALL BUSINESS AND MEDIA ENQUIRIES
steven@perfectchaos.org

ALSO BY STEVEN COLBORNE

The Philosophy of a Mad Man

Ultimate Truth: God Beyond Religion

APPENDIX

The following is a brief excerpt from Steven Colborne's spiritual memoir, *The Philosophy of a Mad Man*, available now.

George's memorial service drew to a close and an old school friend, Chris Jenkins, offered me a lift back to the home of George's family for the reception. Twenty minutes or so later we pulled up and parked a couple of streets along from the house, got out of the car, and began walking up to the house. Other guests were arriving simultaneously, and I struck up conversation with a short and lively lady who was milling around.

After exchanging greetings, conversation quickly turned to George and how each of us knew him. The lady's name was Priscilla. She told me how George had been on a meditation retreat not long before he died, and that she was a member of the same meditation group of which George had been a part.

We began talking about cancer (the cruel illness that had claimed George's life) and I told her a little about my mother's death and her battle with cancer. She began talking about past lives, a subject that felt quite alien to me, and remarked how George had been trampled upon so much in his past lives that even the powerful shaking meditation he had been doing in Bali wasn't able to save his life.

Priscilla described a spiritual experience that she had been going through recently involving being burned at the stake in a past life. She had been a witch. She had had to undergo torturous witch tests like walking barefoot on hot coals – it sounded so fictional and so far removed from any testimony I had ever heard before, and yet she spoke about it with such certainty and truthfulness.

Was I really standing in the presence of a lady who had been a witch in a past life? The thought was quite bewildering, and a little frightening. Priscilla said she'd like to introduce me to a few of her friends. I followed her through George's house into the back garden, where everyone was tucking into sandwiches and drowning memories of George in alcoholic beverages.

Priscilla walked me up to three women who stood together in a semi-circle, eating their lunch. What I saw and felt when I stepped into the presence of these women left me gobsmacked. They seemed to be radiating an immense amount of what I can only describe as light. It was coming from them, and up and around and through them, almost like a force-field. And indeed, it forced me to stand rigid with amazement. I had never seen anything like it.

I exchanged the word "amazing" with one of the women, Sally, for some time (maybe we were amazed by a kind of connection we were all experiencing), and I was so shocked by what was happening that I didn't know where to look, or what to think.

"Wow!" said Sally enthusiastically, as we stood looking into each other's eyes, "a kindred spirit, for sure!" I took these words to be a great compliment, and they lodged firmly in my mind. Perhaps it was a boost to my self-esteem to think that I might be associated with these light-wielding women, and may even be a light-wielding person myself (in spiritual circles there is so much talk of light and enlightenment, and I was truly fascinated by the idea that I might somehow become enlightened).

I got talking to these 'light' women about my mother and about my background with George, and they told me about the shaking meditation they were doing, and how it was a wonderful and powerful way of removing emotional blockages. What they said held resonance with me, as through my mother's battle with cancer I had explored the links between emotional and physical disease in some depth. My mother had introduced me to various proponents of Eastern alternative therapies, Deepak Chopra in particular, with his philosophy that drew on accessing deeper levels of oneself through meditation as a source of healing.

Sally said there was a shaking meditation group in London and that I should come along. It all sounded very exciting! She handed me a small card with a picture of a well-built longhaired Indian man on the front and the words 'Om Swastiastu Ratu Bagus'.

She explained that Ratu was the leader of this shaking meditation practice, and that he had led the retreats in Bali that George attended not long before he died.

Later that evening I went for dinner in a local restaurant with a group of old school friends who had been at the ceremony that day. I tried to engage with the light-hearted conversations about what everyone had been up to and how we all were, but my mind kept flicking back to the 'light' women I had met at the reception, and the shaking practice they had told me about, and the picture of Ratu that I had tucked away in my bag. I was looking forward to the bus journey back home to London that night, when I could be on my own at last to chew over the experiences of the day and ponder what the significance of my introduction to Ratu Bagus might be.

The Philosophy of a Mad Man is out now in paperback and eBook formats

NOTES

About This Book

1. I have not quoted extensively from the Bible, but where I have felt biblical exposition might be of interest to readers, I have added footnotes directing readers to a relevant essay on my free-to-access blog.
2. https://www.youtube.com/c/stevencolborne

1. How Do I Know God Exists?

1. I will elaborate on this argument throughout this book. See, for instance, the chapter entitled "Determinism and the Nature of God" and the later chapter entitled "Cause and Effect".
2. I elaborate on the way in which God talks to human beings in the chapter entitled "Hearing Voices or Hearing God?".
3. I believe the reason why God reveals Himself to some people and not others is that doing so is all part of the plan He has for creation — a plan which I like to describe as God's Grand Game. This concept will be explored in depth in the chapters that follow. Everyone has a role to play in this game, and I believe it's highly likely that everyone will come to the knowledge of God *at some point,* although in many cases this may be after death.

3. What Are God's Attributes?

1. Ontology is the study of the nature of being.
2. I will have more to say about why God causes evil, as well as good, in Part 5.
3. It is possible, however, to speculate on the matter of how God experiences reality, and I have done so in the chapter entitled "Dimensions of Reality".

11. Modes of Mind

1. I realise that we are currently living in what is sometimes described as a 'post-truth' age, where many of the attributes that characterise, for instance, a man and a woman, are being questioned. I take the view that men and women are designed to fit together biologically, although I embrace the idea that members of the LGBTQ+ community all have an important role to play in God's Grand Game. It should be clear from my arguments throughout this book that I believe the attributes of every person, including their sexual preferences, are God-given (and these may, of course, change over time, depending on God's will for the life of each individual). For further reflections in relation to this subject, see the chapter entitled "What is Truth?".
2. The idea that our brains are not the cause of our thoughts is explored in the next chapter.

12. What is Causing Our Thoughts?

1. The idea that our thoughts might be caused by 'subsconcious' activity is criticised in the chapter entitled "Materialism and Free Will".

13. The Experience of Understanding

1. Bryan Magee, *Confessions of a Philosopher* (London: Weidenfeld & Nicolson, 1997), 259.
2. It is also true that God may cause us to forget things as part of the way He unfolds the events of our lives. As God is omniscient, I think it's highly unlikely that God Himself forgets things, although I would accept this as a possibility, especially in the context that God, being eternal, will presumably have an infinite number of things to remember. There is evidence that God has an incredible memory in the regularity that we observe in existence. Consider, for instance, every PIN number and password ever created. God is able to bring them to our minds whenever we need them.

14. Hearing Voices or Hearing God?

1. Steven Colborne, "Some Truths About God," https://perfectchaos.org/2017/08/25/some-truths-about-god/ (last accessed 14th December 2018).
2. For an in-depth discussion of this subject, see my review "'*Neuroscience and Philosophy*' by Bennett, Dennett, Hacker and Searle," at https://perfectchaos.org/2012/03/29/neuroscience-and-philosophy-book-review/ (last accessed 14th December 2018).
3. It is perfectly possible that God uses medication in a way that makes it appear as though they are affecting our mental and physical states. But as I have argued in the chapter entitled "God's Control of Mental States," I believe it is actually God producing the experiences that we attribute to the medications.

15. God's Grand Game

1. Compatibilism (the belief that divine sovereignty and human free will are compatible) is discussed in Part 4.

18. The Confusion of Calvinism

1. *Desiring God* is a Christian ministry run by the American Calvinist John Piper. https://www.desiringgod.org/
2. John Piper, "Does God Control All Things all the Time?," https://www.desiringgod.org/interviews/does-god-control-all-things-all-the-time (last accessed 14th December 2018).
3. Steven Colborne, "An Almighty Predicament: A Discourse on the Arguments For and Against Christianity," https://perfectchaos.org/essays (last accessed 14th December 2018).

19. Molinism Refuted

1. YouTube, "What is Molinism (William Lane Craig)," https://youtu.be/Y-193fhP3mg (last accessed 14th December 2018), (00:00:32).
2. William Lane Craig, "Is Molinism Biblical?," https://www.reasonablefaith.org/media/reasonable-faith-podcast/is-molinism-biblical/ (last accessed 14th December 2018).

21. The Authority of Scripture

1. *Sola scriptura*, literally meaning 'Scripture alone', is a doctrine that came to prominence in the Protestant Reformation of the sixteenth century but is still a staple of Reformed theology today.
2. James R. White, *Scripture Alone: Exploring the Bible's Accuracy, Authority, and Authenticity* (Bloomington, MN: Bethany House Publishers, 2004), 68.
3. Epistemology is the study of how we know what we know.
4. See the chapter entitled "The Experience of Understanding" for further elaboration on the idea that words do not contain intrinsic meaning.

22. What Prayer Reveals About God

1. I expand on this argument in depth in my essay "An Almighty Predicament: A Discourse on the Arguments For and Against Christianity," https://perfectchaos.org/essays (last accessed 14th December 2018).

23. Materialism and Free Will

1. Sam Harris, *Free Will* (New York: Free Press, 2012) (Kindle Version)
2. See, for instance, my book *Ultimate Truth: God Beyond Religion* (Bristol: SilverWood Books, 2013).
3. Harris, *Free Will*, 11.
4. See Harris, *Free Will*, 8 and 20, for example.
5. Harris, *Free Will*, 7.
6. The question of whether our brain controls us or we control

our brain (neither statement being accurate, in my view), is discussed in the earlier chapter entitled "How Do I Know God Exists?".

7. For clarification on what I mean by 'mode of mind', see the chapter entitled "Modes of Mind".

8. For further discussions of these distinct 'dimensions', see the chapter entitled "Dimensions of Reality".

24. The Bible and Free Will

1. I propose some reasons why God might choose to create those things that we consider to be 'evil' in Part 5.

25. Compatibilism

1. Thomas R. Schreiner and Bruce A. Ware, eds., *Still Sovereign: Contemporary Perspectives on Election, Foreknowledge, and Grace* (Grand Rapids, MI: Baker Books, 2000).

2. D. A. Carson, "Reflections on Assurance," in Schreiner and Ware, *Still Sovereign*, 269.

3. Carson, "Reflections on Assurance," in Schreiner and Ware, *Still Sovereign*, 269.

4. Carson, "Reflections on Assurance," in Schreiner and Ware, *Still Sovereign*, 271.

5. For more on the conflict between God's sovereignty and human free will as it relates to the Christian worldview, see my essay "An Almighty Predicament: A Discourse on the Arguments For and Against Christianity," https://perfectchaos.org/essays (last accessed 14th December 2018).

26. Open Theism

1. YouTube, "Greg Boyd on open theism (the open view of the future)," https://youtu.be/SyZQySJeg4g (last accessed 14th December 2018).

27. Divine Conservation and Occasionalism

1. Stanford Encyclopedia of Philosophy, "Creation and Conservation," https://plato.stanford.edu/entries/creation-conservation/ (last accessed 14th December 2018).
2. Southern Evangelical Seminary, "A Window into Christian Philosophy," https://ses.edu/a-window-into-christian-philosophy/ (first accessed 14th December 2018).
3. Internet Encyclopedia of Philosophy, "Occasionalism," https://www.iep.utm.edu/occasion/ (last accessed 14th December 2018).
4. International Society for the Study of Occasionalism, "Occasionalism: A Brief Introduction," http://www.occasionalism.org/an-occasionalist-picture-of-the-universe-islamic-and-cartesian-approaches/ (last accessed 14th December 2018).
5. For evidence of this see the earlier chapter entitled "The Bible and Free Will".

28. Divine Omnipotence and Free Will

1. This attribute of God is discussed further in the chapter entitled "The Aseity of God".

32. Bringing Good out of Evil

1. For more discussion of the areas of theology where interfaith dialogue may be fruitful, see the chapter in Part 7 entitled "Interfaith Dialogue".

33. Do We All Deserve Hell?

1. This is available as a free download from my blog: "An Almighty Predicament: A Discourse on the Arguments For and Against Christianity," https://perfectchaos.org/essays (last accessed 14th December 2018).

37. What is Truth?

1. When I started my philosophy blog in 2012, the reason I decided to call it *Perfect Chaos* was because that phrase accurately describes what I believe is the truth of reality, which is that although activity in the world is seemingly chaotic, God is actually in perfect control of all that unfolds.

38. Creation and Evolution

1. For a definition of falsifiability see Encyclopaedia Britannica, "Criterion of Falsifiability," https://www.britannica.com/topic/criterion-of-falsifiability (last accessed 4th January 2019)
2. Steven Colborne, *The Philosophy of a Mad Man* (Bristol: Silver-Wood Books, 2012), 115–17.

42. Karma

1. This has been explored in depth in the chapter entitled "Cause and Effect".

44. Interfaith Dialogue

1. Confucius, *Analects*, 15:23

INDEX